First Published in 1979 by
Sampson Low, Berkshire House,
Queen Street, Maidenhead,
Berkshire SL6 1NF

SBN 562 00116 6

Designed by Peter Kenny Ltd., Ewell
Filmset by Tradespools Ltd., and Filmtype Services Ltd.
Printed by Waterlows (Dunstable) Ltd.

Sampson Low

Contents

Slimming
MENUS

Cook's guide

In this book, quantities are given in Metric, Imperial and American measures. Where ingredients are differently described in the U.S.A., the alternative name is given in brackets. All menus are to serve 4 unless otherwise indicated.

Spoon measures: In general, teaspoons and tablespoons make handy measures, although not always completely accurate. 3 teaspoons equal 1 tablespoon and 8 tablespoons equal about 150 ml/¼ Imperial pint. (If you use a standard measuring spoon, it actually holds 17.7 ml.) The American tablespoon is slightly smaller (holding 14.2 ml) therefore occasionally an extra tablespoon is indicated in the American column of measures. All spoon measures are taken as being level.

Liquid measures: Quantities are given in millilitres, pints and American cup measures. The American pint contains only 16 fl oz compared with the Imperial pint which contains 20 fl oz, and the American measuring cup contains 8 fl oz.

Can sizes: Since there is no absolute conformity among manufacturers in their can sizes, the exact quantity required is indicated. If, for example, a 396 g/14 oz can of tomatoes is required, the nearest equivalent you can find on the shelves may be up to 50g/2 oz larger or smaller. Generally speaking, this does not affect the success of the recipe.

Oven temperature chart: Few ovens are accurately adjusted. If you are not satisfied with the results given by your oven, test the temperature range with an oven thermometer and set your dial accordingly.

Oven temperature chart

	°F	°C	Gas Mark
Very cool	225	110	¼
	250	130	½
Cool	275	140	1
	300	150	2
Moderate	325	170	3
	350	180	4
Moderately hot	375	190	5
	400	200	6
Hot	425	220	7
	450	230	8
Very hot	475	240	9

Introduction

Many delicious meals are also ideal for slimmers. The menus suggested in this book are for those who have followed a successful diet and want to remain slimmer, fitter and more attractive than in pre-diet days. These appetising dishes will be just as popular with members of the family who have never experienced a weight problem. Yet you might even go on losing weight while eating them if you keep an eye on our calorie chart, only take small portions of the richer foods and exercise restraint when helping yourself to such items as bread and potatoes. Fortunately everyone tends to form better eating habits while dieting and if you can stick to these in principle, lost weight need never creep back. For instance, a starter which includes fruit is not only excellent in itself, but often makes it unnecessary to serve a dessert. Sometimes the thickening agent in a dish can be slightly reduced; so can cream and sugar. Artificial sweeteners are great stand-bys nowadays for slimmers with the proverbial sweet tooth. New low calorie products are constantly being added to the now considerable range which includes salad dressings, fizzy drinks, ketchup and canned fruits. Keep them in stock so that you need never put too heavy a burden on sheer self-control.

Once you have learned how to plan super low calorie meals like these you can enjoy your food as much as anyone and still keep your weight steady.

Audrey Ellis

Calorie counter

The easiest way to check whether what you eat is likely to increase your weight is to estimate your calorie intake. Without doing elaborate sums each time you plan a meal, here are some useful reminders to help you choose foods you enjoy which are reasonably low in calories.

Free cooked vegetables
You may eat as much as you like of the following cooked vegetables seasoned to your taste but without the addition of any butter or sauce:
Artichokes, asparagus, aubergines, bean sprouts, broccoli, Brussels sprouts, cabbage (white, red or green), carrots, cauliflower, celery, chicory, courgettes, leeks, marrow, mushrooms, onions, peppers (red and green), runner beans, spinach, swedes and tomatoes. Small portions only of beetroot, parsnips and peas.

Free salad vegetables
You may eat as much as you like of the following raw salad vegetables, seasoned to your taste with salt and pepper and dressed with natural yogurt, lemon juice or vinegar, or a small quantity of low calorie dressing:
Alfalfa and similar sprouts, bean sprouts, Brussels sprouts, cabbage (white, red and green), carrots, cauliflower, celery, chicory, Chinese leaves, cucumber, endive, leeks, lettuce, mushrooms, mustard and cress, onions, parsley, peppers (red and green), radishes, spinach, spring onions, tomatoes and watercress.

Fruit
Since confectionary, biscuits and cakes are relatively high in calories, try to eat fresh raw fruit as often as possible instead. Citrus fruits such as oranges and grapefruits are lowest in calorie value, berry fruits such as raspberries and strawberries come next, then stone fruits such as plums and greengages and hard fruits such as apples and pears. Exotic fruit such as bananas and mangoes are highest. Cooked fruit which is sweetened with sugar is higher in calories but if it is sweetened after cooking with an artificial sweetener it can be counted as fresh fruit.

Drinks
You probably consume more calories than you realise in the form of drinks. Substitute skimmed milk for whole milk whenever possible. Low calorie mixer drinks are easily available and dry white wine is the most acceptable choice for slimmers when dining out and wishing to drink alcohol.

Calorie chart

Food	Quantity	Calorie Count
Anchovy, drained	1 fillet	7
Apple, 1 small		40
Apple purée, sweetened	125 ml/4 fl oz	100
Apricot, 1 medium		15
Artichoke, globe	1 globe	12
Jerusalem	100 g/4 oz	20
Asparagus	100 g/4 oz	20
Avocado	½ pear	125
Bacon, lean, grilled (broiled)	25 g/1 oz	75
Beans, baked in tomato sauce	100 g/4 oz	100
broad	100 g/4 oz	55
green	100 g/4 oz	25
Bean sprouts	100 g/4 oz	32
Beef, cooked, lean	25 g/1 oz	75
Beetroot	100 g/4 oz	40
Biscuits, (crackers) cream crackers	2	70
(cookies) semi-sweet	2	60
Blackberries	100 g/4 oz	40
Blackcurrants	100 g/4 oz	40
Bread, white	25 g /1 oz	70
Breakfast cereals, average	25 g/1 oz	100
Broccoli	100 g/4 oz	40
Brussels sprouts	100 g/4 oz	25
Butter	25 g/1 oz/ 2 tbspns	220
Cabbage	100 g/4 oz	20
Carrots	100 g/4 oz	20
Cauliflower	100 g/4 oz	20
Celery	100 g/4 oz	15
Cheese, hard	25 g/1 oz	100
curd (farmer)	50 g/2 oz	75
Cherries	12	40
Chicken, cooked	25 g/1 oz	30
Chicory (Belgian endive)	1 head	6
Chocolate, average	25 g/1 oz	150
Cider, average	300 ml/ ½ pint/1¼ cups	100
Coconut	25 g/1 oz	170
Coffee	—	neg.
Corn salad	4 leaves	neg.
Courgettes (zucchini)	100 g/4 oz	20
Crabmeat	100 g/4 oz	120
Cream, single (half & half)	1 tbspn	25
double (whipping)	1 tbspn	50
Crispbread	thin-thick	15-35

Food	Quantity	Calorie Count
Cucumber	100 g/4 oz	20
Egg, whole, poached or boiled	1	75
white only		15
yolk only		60
Fish, white – cod, haddock, plaice, etc.	25 g/1 oz	30
oily – herring, mackerel, trout	25 g/1 oz	50
Flour, white	100 g/4 oz 1 cup	450
wholemeal	100 g/4 oz/ 1 cup	400
Fruit salad, fresh	100 g/4 oz	40
canned	100 g/4 oz	90
Gammon, (uncooked ham) lean	25 g/1 oz	75
Gelatine, unflavoured	25 g/1 oz	70
Gooseberries	100 g/4 oz	40
Grapes, black	100 g/4 oz	56
white	100 g/4 oz	68
Grapefruit	1 half	15
juice, unsweetened	125 ml/4 fl oz/ ½ cup	40
Gravy, home-made	1 tbspn	15
Ham, lean	25 g/1 oz	75
Honey	1 tbspn	65
Ice cream, average	100 g/4 oz	300
Jam	1 tbspn	55
Kidney	25 g/1 oz	34
Lamb, cooked, lean	25 g/1 oz	75
Lemon	1 medium	20
juice	1 tbspn	5
Lettuce	4 leaves	neg.
Liver	25 g/1 oz	40
Lobster meat	25 g/1 oz	34
Macaroni, cooked	50 g/2 oz	64
Margarine	25 g/1 oz 2 tbspns	210
Marmalade	1 tbspn	55
Marrow	100 g/4 oz	10
Melon, average	100 g/4 oz	20
Milk, skimmed	125 ml/4 fl oz/ ½ cup	40
whole	125 ml/4 fl oz/ ½ cup	80
Nuts, shelled, average	25 g/1 oz	160
Oil, cooking, average	25 ml/1 fl oz	255

Food	Quantity	Calorie Count
Olives	each	7
Onion	100 g/4 oz	25
Orange	1 medium	40
juice, unsweetened	125 ml/4 fl oz/ ½ cup	40
Parsley	25 g/1 oz	5
Parsnip	100 g/4 oz	55
Pasta, cooked	50 g/2 oz	64
Pastry, average	25 g/1 oz	125
Paw paw	½ fruit	50
Peach	1 medium	36
Pear	1 medium	40
Peas, shelled	100 g/4 oz	70
dried	100 g/4 oz	110
Peppers	1 medium	20
Pheasant, cooked	25 g/1 oz	60
Pickles, clear mixed	1 tbspn	neg.
sweet	1 tbspn	55
Pilchard, canned	25 g/1 oz	55
Pineapple, fresh	100 g/4 oz	55
juice	125 ml/4 fl oz/ ½ cup	55
Plums	1 large	20
Pork, cooked, lean	25 g/1 oz	75
Potatoes, boiled or baked	100 g/4 oz	90
fried	100 g/4 oz	280
mashed	100 g/4 oz	120
roast	100 g/4 oz	140
Prawns (shrimp), shelled	25 g/1 oz	30
Prunes	2 medium	40
Rabbit, on bone	25 g/1 oz	37
Radishes	3 medium	5
Raspberries	100 g/4 oz	32
Rhubarb (unsweetened)	100 g/4 oz	16
Rice, cooked	100 g/4 oz	140
Salad cream (dressing)	1 tbspn	50
Salmon	25 g/1 oz	50
Sardines, canned in oil	3 medium	150
Sauce, white	125 ml/4 fl oz/ ½ cup	160
cheese	125 ml/4 fl oz/ ½ cup	250
sweet	125 ml/4 fl oz/ ½ cup	200
Sausage (Beef or Pork links), cooked	1 small	75

Food	Quantity	Calorie Count
Shrimps, shelled	25 g/1 oz	32
Soups, clear	300 ml/½ pint/ 1¼ cups	60
cream	300 ml/½ pint/ 1¼ cups	150
mixed vegetable	300 ml/½ pint/ 1¼ cups	100
Spinach	100 g/4 oz	20
Spring greens	100 g/4 oz	16
Steak, lean	25 g/1 oz	50
Stock (broth)	125 ml/4 fl oz/ ½ cup	4
(bouillon) cube (beef or chicken)	1 cube	15
Strawberries	100 g/4 oz	32
Stuffing, (bread)	25 g/1 oz	100
Sugar	25 g/1 oz/ 2 tbspns	110
Swede (rutabaga)	100 g/4 oz	20
Sweetcorn kernels	100 g/4 oz	80
Sweets (candies), average	25 g/1 oz	100
Syrup, golden (corn)	25 g/1 oz/ 1 tbspn	85
Tangerine	1 medium	40
Tea	—	neg.
Tomatoes	1 medium	20
Tongue, cooked	25 g/1 oz	75
Tripe	25 g/1 oz	30
Turkey, cooked	25 g/1 oz	30
Tuna, canned, drained	25 g/1 oz	75
Turnips	100 g/4 oz	20
Veal	25 g/1 oz	50
Vinegar	1 tbspn	neg.
Watercress	4 sprigs	neg.
Wine, dry	125 ml/4 fl oz/ ½ cup	76
sweet	125 ml/4 fl oz/ ½ cup	100
Yogurt, natural (plain)	125 ml/4 fl oz/ ½ cup	90
Yorkshire (batter) pudding	25 g/1 oz	60

Vegetables are measured cooked and drained where applicable.
Meat and fish are raw unless otherwise stated.

Most of these meal plans include three courses but if a quick calorie count suggests to you that you should omit one course, it is usually easiest to do without the dessert. No recipes are given for simple courses in the menus, such as fresh fruit salad. The menus are in each case for the main meal of the day and for dieters other meals should be snacks, much lower in calories, such as cottage cheese with crispbreads and tomatoes.

Whiting with anchovy and caper dressing
Rice and avocado salad
Pineapple mousse

Whiting with anchovy and caper dressing

INGREDIENTS	METRIC	IMP.	U.S.
Whiting or other white fish fillets	*750 g*	*1½ lb*	*1½ lb*
Salt and black pepper			
Butter	*50 g*	*2 oz*	*¼ cup*
4 spring onions [scallions]			
Canned anchovy fillets	*50 g*	*2 oz*	*2 oz*
2 tbspns capers			
Grated rind and juice of ½ lemon			
1 tbspn chopped parsley			

Season the fish with salt and pepper. Steam between two plates over a pan of simmering water for about 20 minutes, until just cooked and milky white. Just before the fish is cooked, melt the butter in a small pan. Chop the onions, add to the pan and fry for about 1 minute without browning. Drain and chop the anchovies and capers and add to the pan with the lemon rind and juice. Stir over heat until the mixture boils. Place the fish on a hot serving dish and spoon over the dressing. Sprinkle with parsley.

Rice and avocado salad

INGREDIENTS	METRIC	IMP.	U.S.
Long grain rice	*175 g*	*6 oz*	*¾ cup*
Natural [plain] yogurt	*150 ml*	*5 fl oz*	*½ cup +*
French [Italian] dressing	*100 ml*	*3 fl oz*	*½ cup –*
Good pinch ground nutmeg			
4 small tomatoes			
Diced cucumber	*100 g*	*4 oz*	*⅔ cup*
Diced cheese	*100 g*	*4 oz*	*⅔ cup*
2 avocados			
1 tbspn lemon juice			
Sprig of parsley			

Cook the rice in plenty of boiling salted water until just tender. Turn into a colander and run fresh boiling water through it. Combine the natural (plain) yogurt, French dressing and nutmeg to taste. Toss the well drained rice in this dressing while still warm enough to absorb it slightly. Dice the tomatoes, discarding the seeds, and fold into the rice with cucumber and cheese. Peel the avocados, cut in half. Remove stones and dice one avocado, cut the other into eight slices lengthways. Toss in the lemon juice, add the diced avocado to the salad, turn into a bowl and decorate with avocado slices and parsley.

Pineapple mousse

INGREDIENTS	METRIC	IMP.	U.S.
Unsweetened pineapple juice	*450 ml*	*¾ pint*	*2 cups*
1 tbspn gelatine [gelatin]			
8 marshmallows			
2 egg whites			

Place the pineapple juice in a saucepan with the gelatine. Stir over moderate heat until the gelatine has dissolved. Add the marshmallows and continue stirring until the mixture is smooth. Cool, stirring occasionally, until beginning to set, then whisk until frothy. Stiffly whisk the egg whites and fold into the pineapple mixture. Divide between 4 dishes and allow to set.

SASSO

Crab and shrimp bisque
Piquant veal escalopes
Petits pois
Fresh fruit salad

Crab and shrimp bisque

INGREDIENTS	METRIC	IMP.	U.S.
1 slice streaky [side] bacon			
1 small onion			
Tomatoes	*450 g*	*1 lb*	*1 lb*
Chicken stock [broth]	*600 ml*	*1 pint*	*$2\frac{1}{2}$ cups*
Peeled shrimps	*100 g*	*4 oz*	*$\frac{2}{3}$ cup*
Crabmeat	*100 g*	*4 oz*	*$\frac{1}{2}$ cup*
Salt and pepper			
Lemon juice			
Single cream [half & half]	*150 ml*	*$\frac{1}{4}$ pint*	*$\frac{1}{2}$ cup*

Dice the bacon and fry until the fat runs. Chop the onion and fry in the bacon fat until limp. Skin and deseed the tomatoes. Add the tomato flesh and chicken stock to the onion and bacon. Simmer for 10 minutes. Sieve or liquidise in a blender. Return to the saucepan and stir in the shrimps and crabmeat. Add salt, pepper and lemon juice to taste. Reheat, then stir in the cream. This soup may be served hot or cold.

Note: **A slimmer's portion may be finished with skimmed milk instead of cream.**

Piquant veal escalopes

INGREDIENTS	METRIC	IMP.	U.S.
4 escalopes of veal			
Seasoned flour for coating			
Butter	*75 g*	*3 oz*	*6 tbspns*
6 chopped spring onions [scallions]			
1 sliced lemon			
2 tspns dried rosemary			
Salt and freshly ground black pepper			
$\frac{1}{4}$ tspn Tabasco pepper sauce			
Dry vermouth	*150 ml*	*$\frac{1}{4}$ pint*	*$\frac{1}{2}$ cup*
1 tbspn chopped parsley			

Bat out the escalopes thinly and cut each in half. Dust with seasoned flour. Quickly fry them in 2 oz/50 g of the butter until golden. Remove and keep warm. Fry the white part of the spring onions in the remaining butter until soft. Replace the veal and add the lemon slices, rosemary, seasoning, Tabasco, vermouth and green part of the spring onions. Cook for a further 2-3 minutes. Arrange on a serving dish and garnish with the chopped parsley.

Spiced tomato cocktail
Avocado and salmon mousse
Lettuce salad with mayonnaise
Grapes in nectar

Spiced tomato cocktail

INGREDIENTS	METRIC	IMP.	U.S.
Ripe tomatoes	*450 g*	*1 lb*	*1 lb*
1 small onion			
1 stalk celery			
1 tbspn sugar			
1 tspn salt			
$\frac{1}{4}$ tspn pepper			
3 whole cloves			
Pinch ground ginger			
Water	*50 ml*	*2 fl oz*	*$\frac{1}{4}$ cup*
2 tbspns lemon juice			
1 tbspn white vinegar			

Chop the tomatoes, onion and celery stalk. Add the remaining ingredients and simmer until the vegetables are tender. Pass through a strainer, discarding the pulp. Refrigerate the juice until serving time, or put in cubes of ice. Serve in tall glasses with curls of lemon rind hanging over the edges.

Fruit flavoured mayonnaises are lighter in texture than the classic type. Squeeze a little juice from the citrus fruit of your choice, strain and use instead of vinegar when making the mayonnaise. With sweet orange juice you may need a teaspoon of vinegar as well. Add only sufficient oil to make the texture fluffy, not stiff. Fold a little grated rind from the fruit into the mayonnaise and sprinkle more on top in the sauceboat. Slimmers' salad dressings are more interesting with an added touch of orange or lemon flavour too.

Avocado and salmon mousse

INGREDIENTS	METRIC	IMP.	U.S.
Cooked fresh or canned salmon	*225 g*	*8 oz*	*½ lb*
Unflavoured gelatine [gelatin]	*15 g*	*½ oz*	*1 tbspn*
2 avocado pears			
½ tspn salt			
Pinch white pepper			
2 tspns anchovy essence [extract]			
3 tbspns single cream [half & half]			
Few drops green food colouring			
2 egg whites			
1 stuffed green olive and parsley to garnish			

Drain the salmon, reserving the juice, or a little cooking liquid, remove the bones and skin and flake the flesh. Dissolve the gelatine in 3 tablespoons hot water. Cut the avocados in half lengthwise, remove the stones and skin and cut the flesh into pieces. Liquidise the avocado, salt, pepper, anchovy essence and the salmon juice in a blender, until smooth, or mash thoroughly with a fork and then beat until smooth. Place in a fairly large bowl, stir in the dissolved gelatine, the cream and the flaked salmon, adding a little green food colouring. Whisk the egg whites until just holding their shape, then using a metal spoon fold into the salmon mixture. Turn into a rinsed fish mould or ring mould and leave to set. Turn out on to a serving platter and garnish with olive slices and parsley. Serve with prawns, or a salad garnish.

Grapes in nectar

INGREDIENTS	METRIC	IMP.	U.S.
Green grapes	*225 g*	*8 oz*	*½ lb*
Black [purple] grapes	*225 g*	*8 oz*	*½ lb*
1 tspn lemon juice			
4 tbspns clear honey			
2 tbspns sweet sherry			
Toasted flaked [slivered] almonds	*25 g*	*1 oz*	*¼ cup*

Halve and deseed the grapes and place in a basin. Mix together the lemon juice, honey and sherry and pour over the grapes. Allow to stand at room temperature for at least 2 hours, then chill until required. Spoon into tall glasses and decorate each with a sprinkling of toasted flaked almonds.

Carrot soup
Turkey with glazed chicory
Orange and grapefruit jellied cheesecake

Carrot soup

INGREDIENTS	METRIC	IMP.	U.S.
1 large onion			
1 large potato			
2 cloves garlic			
Carrots	*575 g*	*$1\frac{1}{4}$ lb*	*$1\frac{1}{4}$ lb*
Butter	*25 g*	*1 oz*	*2 tbspns*
2 chicken stock [bouillon] cubes			
Boiling water	*900 ml*	*$1\frac{1}{2}$ pints*	*$3\frac{3}{4}$ cups*
1 tspn cornflour [cornstarch]			
Natural [plain] Yogurt	*150 ml*	*$\frac{1}{4}$ pint*	*$\frac{2}{3}$ cup*
Salt and pepper			
1 tspn finely grated lemon rind			

Slice the onion and potato and crush the garlic. Grate the carrots. Melt the butter and use to cook the onion and garlic until soft. Add the carrot and potato and cook for about 6 minutes. Dissolve the stock cubes in the boiling water. Add to the pan and bring to the boil. Cover and simmer for about 30 minutes. Moisten the cornflour with a tablespoon of water and add to the yogurt in a small saucepan. Bring to the boil, stirring constantly, and cook for 2 minutes. Liquidise or sieve the two mixtures together and return to the pan. Reheat, adjust seasoning and serve garnished with grated lemon rind.

Turkey with glazed chicory

INGREDIENTS	METRIC	IMP.	U.S.
Chicory [Belgian endive], trimmed	*450 g*	*1 lb*	*1 lb*
1 tbspn vinegar			
Cooked turkey, chopped	*450 g*	*1 lb*	*1 lb*
Canned tomatoes	*227 g*	*8 oz*	*1 cup*
Butter	*25 g*	*1 oz*	*2 tbspns*
Demerara [brown] sugar	*25 g*	*1 oz*	*2 tbspns*
½ tspn dried oregano			
Salt and pepper			

Cook the chicory heads in boiling salted water until just tender but not soft, adding the vinegar to avoid discolouration. Drain, mix with the turkey, place in an ovenproof serving dish. Heat the tomatoes with the butter, sugar, herbs and seasoning to taste and simmer for 3 minutes. Sieve and pour over the chicory, to coat well. Place in a moderately hot oven (375°F, 190°C, Gas Mark 5) for about 15 minutes.

Orange and grapefruit jellied cheesecake

INGREDIENTS	METRIC	IMP.	U.S.
1 lemon jelly [package lemon flavored gelatin]			
3 grapefruits			
3 oranges			
3 eggs			
Castor [granulated] sugar	*50 g*	*2 oz*	*¼ cup*
Milk	*450 ml*	*¾ pint*	*2 cups*
Few drops vanilla essence [extract]			
1 tbspn gelatine [gelatin]			
3 tbspns water			
'Philly' soft cheese	*75 g*	*3 oz*	*3 oz*
Double [whipping] cream	*125 ml*	*4 fl oz*	*½ cup*

Make up the jelly to 450 ml/¾ pint/2 cups with boiling water. Pour a little into a 20-cm/8-inch cake tin and allow to set. Peel and segment the grapefruits and oranges. Dip segments in jelly and arrange in cake tin. Spoon over the rest of the jelly. Chill. Whisk the eggs with the sugar. Heat the milk until almost boiling, pour on to the egg mixture and whisk well. Strain into a double saucepan and cook over boiling water until the custard will coat the back of a spoon. Flavour with vanilla and cool. Dissolve the gelatine in the water in a basin over a pan of hot water. Cream the cheese, and gradually beat in the cooled custard and dissolved gelatine. Whip the cream, fold into the cheese mixture and pour into the tin. Allow to set. Dip tin in hot water, turn out on a serving dish. If wished, reserve a little of the cream to decorate the cheesecake.

Melon and cheese starters
Salmon in aspic with artichoke salad

Melon and cheese starters

INGREDIENTS	METRIC	IMP.	U.S.
2 Ogen [small cantaloupe] melons			
Cooked French [green] beans	*100 g*	*4 oz*	$\frac{1}{4}$ *lb*
2 tbspns French [Italian] dressing			
Cheddar cheese, diced	*100 g*	*4 oz*	$\frac{1}{4}$ *lb*
4 radishes			

Cut the melons in half across and scoop out the seeds. With a melon baller, remove about 4 balls from each melon half. Cut the beans into short lengths, toss with the melon balls in the French dressing. Pile up with the cheese dice in the melon halves. Top each with a radish rose.

Salmon in aspic with artichoke salad

INGREDIENTS	METRIC	IMP.	U.S.
4 thin slices salmon			
$\frac{1}{2}$ tspn salt			
Water	*300 ml*	*$\frac{1}{2}$ pint*	*$1\frac{1}{4}$ cups*
2 tspns unflavoured gelatine [gelatin]			
4 cooked artichoke bottoms			
4 cooked new potatoes			
2 cooked carrots			
1 lemon			
Mayonnaise	*150 ml*	*$\frac{1}{4}$ pint*	*$\frac{2}{3}$ cup*
Few lettuce leaves			
1 hard-boiled egg and a few black and stuffed green olives to garnish			

Poach the salmon slices in the salted water until tender. Drain and allow to cool. Reduce the poaching liquid to $\frac{1}{4}$ pint/150 ml/$\frac{1}{2}$ cup. Moisten the gelatine in 2 tablespoons water and stir into the warm liquid until dissolved. Pour the jelly over the salmon slices when it becomes syrupy. Allow to set. Meanwhile, chop the artichoke bottoms, potatoes and carrots. Squeeze the juice from half the lemon and add to the mayonnaise. Cut the other lemon half into slices. Fold the vegetables into the lemon mayonnaise. Place a few lettuce leaves on a serving platter and arrange the glazed salmon slices and vegetable salad on top. Garnish with slices of egg and lemon, and the olives.

Clear beetroot soup
Sweetcorn and crab salad
Jellied veal with lettuce hearts

Clear beetroot soup

INGREDIENTS	METRIC	IMP.	U.S.
1 large raw beetroot [beet]			
Beef stock [broth]	*1.5 litres*	*2½ pints*	*6 cups*
1 large carrot, grated			
1 large onion, chopped			
Salt and pepper			
1 tspn dried dill weed or 1 tbspn chopped fresh dill			

Peel the beetroot, chop a little of it into neat dice and reserve for the garnish. Grate the remainder coarsely and place in a saucepan with the stock and other vegetables. Cover and simmer for 25-30 minutes, until all the vegetables are very tender. Taste and correct the seasoning. Strain, add the diced beetroot and cook for 8 minutes. Serve sprinkled with dill. Serves 6.

Sweetcorn and crab salad

INGREDIENTS	METRIC	IMP.	U.S.
1 small red pepper			
1 large cooked crab			
Cooked long grain rice	*100 g*	*4 oz*	*1 cup*
2 tbspns mayonnaise			
Cooked sweetcorn kernels	*225 g*	*8 oz*	*1 cup*
1 tbspn chopped chives			
DRESSING			
2 tbspns lemon juice			
½ tspn salt			
¼ tspn white pepper			
½ tspn castor [granulated] sugar			
4 tbspns corn oil			

First make the dressing. Beat together the lemon juice, seasoning and sugar and gradually add the oil. Deseed and cut the pepper into strips. Marinate in the dressing for at least 2 hours. Remove the flesh from the crab and reserve the claw meat. Mix the remaining crab meat lightly with the rice and mayonnaise and place in a shallow serving dish. Toss the chunks of claw meat, corn kernels, red pepper strips and chives together in the dressing and arrange over the rice mixture. Serve chilled. Serves 6.

Jellied veal

INGREDIENTS	METRIC	IMP.	U.S.
Pie veal	*1 kg*	*2 lb*	*2 lb*
2 tbspns oil			
Sprig of rosemary			
Sprig of thyme			
1 bay leaf			
Salt and pepper			
Water	*300 ml*	*½ pint*	*1¼ cups*
Dry white wine	*300 ml*	*½ pint*	*1¼ cups*
6 small carrots, sliced			
1 egg white and shell			
Liquid aspic, made with veal stock	*600 ml*	*1 pint*	*2½ cups*
2 tomatoes, quartered			
Sprigs of parsley			

Cut the meat into large dice. Toss in the hot oil to seal. Add the herbs, salt, pepper, water and wine and cook, covered, over gentle heat for 45 minutes. Add the carrots and cook for a further 15 minutes. Remove and reserve the meat and carrots. Strain the remaining stock and bring to the boil with the lightly beaten egg white and the shell. When completely clear, strain off shell. Add the aspic jelly and if necessary make up to 1½ pint/scant 1 litre/3¾ cups with more water. Pour a little stock into the base of an 8 inch/20 cm mould or cake tin. When set, arrange carrot rings decoratively round base and sides, add half the meat and pour in half the stock. Chill until firm. Add the remaining meat, carrots and stock and chill until set. Loosen edges with a knife, dip base of mould into hot water and turn out on a serving dish. Decorate with tomato wedges and parsley sprigs. Serves 6.

Individual lettuce heart salads are easy and cheap to prepare in summer and make a change from the usual leafy salad. Buy pale greenish-gold hearts or use the hearts only from several lettuces. Quarter and wash well without tearing apart. Drain carefully on soft kitchen paper. Arrange the quarters opened out on a basis of cucumber slices, or on one large lettuce leaf. Sprinkle lightly with French (Italian) dressing, then with finely chopped parsley and chives. Place a radish rose in the centre and between the quarters.

Salmon mousse with olives
Chicken and melon salad
Apricot fluff

Salmon mousse with olives

INGREDIENTS	METRIC	IMP.	U.S.
1 chicken stock [bouillon] cube			
Boiling water	*300 ml*	$\frac{1}{2}$ *pint*	$1\frac{1}{4}$ *cups*
1 tbspn gelatine [gelatin]			
30 stuffed green olives			
Milk	*300 ml*	$\frac{1}{2}$ *pint*	$1\frac{1}{4}$ *cups*
2 bay leaves			
1 small onion			
Butter	*40 g*	$1\frac{1}{2}$ *oz*	*3 tbspns*
Flour	*40 g*	$1\frac{1}{2}$ *oz*	*6 tbspns*
Canned red salmon	*215 g*	$7\frac{1}{2}$ *oz*	$7\frac{1}{2}$ *oz*
2 tbspns mayonnaise			
Grated rind of 1 lemon			
Salt and freshly ground pepper			

Make up stock cube with water. Stir in gelatine until completely dissolved. Cool. Pour a thin layer into a 20-cm/8-inch cake tin. Slice the olives and arrange a few in the tin. Spoon in a little more of the gelatine mixture. Chill. Heat the milk to boiling point with the bay leaves and onion. Stand for 5 minutes. Melt the butter, stir in the flour and gradually add the strained milk. Bring to the boil, stirring constantly, until smooth and thick. Remove bones from salmon and flake finely. Stir into sauce with liquid from can, mayonnaise, lemon rind and remaining jellied stock. Season with salt and pepper. Arrange a ring of olive slices around the side of the tin, pour in half the salmon mixture then add another ring of olive slices and the remaining mixture. Smooth the top and chill until set. Dip tin in hot water and turn out on a serving dish.

Chicken and melon salad

INGREDIENTS	METRIC	IMP.	U.S.
Boiled new potatoes	*450 g*	*1 lb*	*1 lb*
Cooked chicken	*225 g*	*8 oz*	*½ lb*
Diced melon flesh	*225 g*	*8 oz*	*1 cup*
1 tbspn salad cream [dressing]			
1 tbspn oil			
2 tbspns white vinegar			
2 tbspns finely chopped mint			
Salt and pepper			
Lettuce leaves			
Tomato wedges			
1 mint sprig			

Cut the potatoes and chicken into neat pieces and place in a bowl with the melon. Mix together the salad cream, oil, vinegar, chopped mint and seasoning in a screw-topped jar and shake well. Pour over the chicken mixture and toss lightly. Arrange a bed of lettuce leaves on a serving dish, top with the chicken salad and garnish with wedges of tomato. Top with the mint sprig and serve straight away.

Apricot fluff

INGREDIENTS	METRIC	IMP.	U.S.
Ripe apricots	*225 g*	*8 oz*	*½ lb*
6 tbspns water			
1 tbspn gelatine [gelatin]			
Natural [plain] yogurt	*150 ml*	*¼ pint*	*½ cup*
2 egg whites			

Halve and stone the apricots and cook with 4 tablespoons water until soft. Liquidize in a blender until smooth and sweeten to taste. Dissolve the gelatine in 2 tablespoons water in a basin over a pan of hot water. Stir gelatine into the purée with the yogurt. When the mixture starts to thicken, fold in the egg whites, stiffly-whisked. Divide between 4 dishes and chill until set. (For slimmers, use liquid sweetener.)

Lamb cutlets with pawpaw salad
Cauliflower in chicken cream
Red wine jelly

Lamb cutlets with pawpaw salad

INGREDIENTS	METRIC	IMP.	U.S.
1 pawpaw			
12 spring onions [scallions]			
8 lamb cutlets			
2 tbspns oil			
Butter	*25 g*	*1 oz*	*2 tbspns*
Salt and pepper			
1 tspn chopped mint			

Cut the pawpaw in half, remove the seeds and skin and cut the flesh into $\frac{1}{4}$ inch/$\frac{1}{2}$ cm cubes. Trim the onions, leaving about 2 inches/5 cm of the green top. Brush the cutlets on both sides with the oil and grill under moderate heat for about 10 minutes, turning once. Meanwhile, melt the butter in a shallow pan, add the pawpaw, onions and seasonings. Cover and simmer for 5-10 minutes while the cutlets are cooking. Place the pawpaw mixture on a serving dish, sprinkle with chopped mint and surround with the cutlets.

Cauliflower in chicken cream

INGREDIENTS	METRIC	IMP.	U.S.
Milk	*450 ml*	*¾ pint*	*2 cups*
1 bay leaf			
1 chicken stock [bouillon] cube			
1 large cauliflower			
Butter	*75 g*	*3 oz*	*⅓ cup*
Flour	*40 g*	*1½ oz*	*⅓ cup*
1 tbspn lemon juice			
Grated cheese	*50 g*	*2 oz*	*½ cup*
Double [whipping] cream, whipped	*4 tbspns*	*4 tbspns*	*⅓ cup*
1 tbspn oil			
Soft breadcrumbs	*75 g*	*3 oz*	*1 cup*
Salt and pepper			
1 tspn finely grated lemon rind			

Warm the milk with the bay leaf and dissolve the stock cube in it. Allow to stand for 20 minutes. Meanwhile, cook the cauliflower whole in plenty of salted boiling water, drain and turn out carefully into a colander, invert on to a warm serving dish and keep hot. While the cauliflower is cooking, make the sauce and prepare the crumb topping. Melt half the butter, stir in the flour and cook for 2 minutes. Gradually strain in the seasoned milk, bring to the boil and whisk until smooth. Cook for 1 minute. Add the lemon juice and finally the grated cheese. As soon as the cheese is melted, stir in the cream and pour sauce over the cauliflower. Heat the remaining butter with the oil and use to fry the breadcrumbs golden brown. Season with salt and pepper, stir in the lemon rind and sprinkle over and round the cauliflower.

Red wine jelly

INGREDIENTS	METRIC	IMP.	U.S.
Red wine	*450 ml*	*¾ pint*	*2 cups*
Pinch each ground cinnamon, nutmeg and ginger			
1 clove			
Little sugar			
1 tbspn gelatine [gelatin]			
Whipped cream for decoration			

Place red wine in a pan with the spices. Bring to boiling point and boil rapidly for 4 minutes to reduce. Add sugar to taste and cool. Dissolve the gelatine in 2 tablespoons water in a basin over a pan of hot water. Strain in the spiced wine and stir well. Divide between 4 wine glasses and allow to set. Decorate each dessert with a small rosette of whipped cream.

Avocado pears with fire 'n ice tomatoes
Baked whole plaice with buttered rice
Cucumber and celery salad
Peach and strawberry flambé

Avocado pears with fire'n ice tomatoes

INGREDIENTS	METRIC	IMP.	U.S.
4 tomatoes			
1 onion			
4 ice cubes			
White vinegar	*125 ml*	*4 fl oz*	*½ cup*
1 tspn celery seed			
½ tspn salt			
¼ tspn dry mustard			
Pinch cayenne pepper			
¼ tspn freshly ground black pepper			
1 tbspn sugar			
2 avocado pears			

Peel and slice the tomatoes and slice the onion. Place these in alternate layers in a deep bowl and add the ice cubes. Combine the vinegar, seasonings and sugar in a small saucepan and boil for 1 minute. Pour over the tomatoes and onion and chill until serving time. Peel and dice the avocado pears. Divide among 4 serving dishes. Drain the tomato and onion mixture and spoon over the avocado.

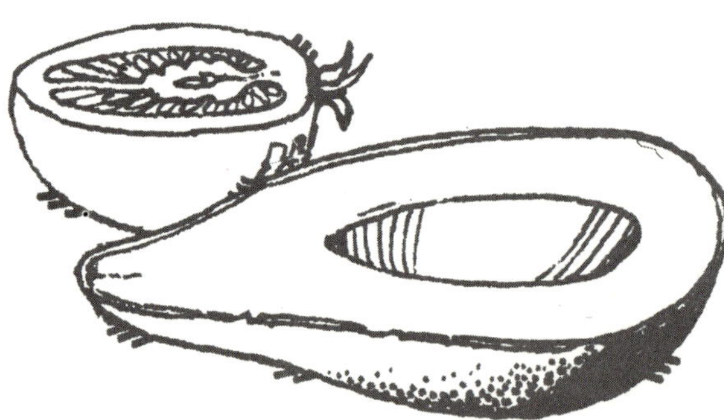

Baked whole plaice with buttered rice

INGREDIENTS	METRIC	IMP.	U.S.
Butter	*100 g*	*4 oz*	*½ cup*
1 whole plaice	*1.5 kg*	*3 lb*	*3 lb*
Salt and pepper			
1 large onion			
4 lemons			
Chopped parsley			
BUTTERED RICE			
Long grain rice	*225 g*	*8 oz*	*1 cup*
1 tspn salt			
Boiling water	*600 ml*	*1 pint*	*2½ cups*
2 hard-boiled egg yolks			
Butter	*25 g*	*1 oz*	*2 tbspns*

First prepare the buttered rice. Place the rice and salt in an ovenproof dish, pour over the boiling water and stir well. Cover and cook in a moderately hot oven (375°F, 190°C, Gas Mark 5) for about 40 minutes, until the rice is tender and the liquid absorbed. Meanwhile, butter a large shallow ovenproof dish with some of the 100 g/4 oz/½ cup of butter. Put in the fish and season well. Slice the onion and the lemons. Top the fish with all the onion slices and some of the lemon slices. Dot with remaining butter. Cook in the oven with the rice for about 45 minutes, until the fish flakes easily when tested with a fork. Remove the onion and lemon slices and the skin from the fish. Garnish with the remaining lemon slices and a little parsley. Fluff up the rice, mash the egg yolks and stir into the rice with the butter. Sprinkle with parsley and serve with the baked plaice.

Peach and strawberry flambé

INGREDIENTS	METRIC	IMP.	U.S.
4 fresh peaches			
Water	*600 ml*	*1 pint*	*2½ cups*
Sugar	*100 g*	*4 oz*	*½ cup*
1 long strip lemon rind			
¼ stick cinnamon			
Fresh strawberries	*225 g*	*8 oz*	*½ lb*
1 tspn grated orange rind			
Brandy	*50 ml*	*2 fl oz*	*¼ cup*

Place the unpeeled peaches in a saucepan. Combine the water and sugar and pour over the peaches. Add the lemon rind and cinnamon stick. Bring to the boil and simmer 15 minutes. Take out the peaches, skin, cut in half and remove the stones. Place the peach halves, cut side down, in a chafing dish. Crush the strawberries, add the orange rind and ¼ pint/150 ml/ ½ cup of peach syrup. Pour over the peaches and heat gently. Warm the brandy, pour into the chafing dish and light with a match. Serve immediately with cream or over vanilla ice cream.

Breton fish salad
Celery in rich tomato
Fresh fruit basket

Breton fish salad

INGREDIENTS	METRIC	IMP.	U.S.
4 scallops in the shell			
Dry white wine	*300 ml*	*½ pint*	*1¼ cups*
Salt and pepper			
Mussels	*½ litre+*	*1 pint*	*2½ cups*
Prawns	*100 g*	*4 oz*	*¼ lb*
4 tbspns French [Italian] dressing			
4 medium new potatoes			
2 tbspns chopped chives			

Remove scallops from the shells and place in a saucepan. Cover with the wine, season and bring to the boil. Reduce the heat and poach for 5 minutes. Drain and dice the scallops. Use up the poaching liquid to cook the mussels, having first removed the beards, until they open. Remove mussels from shells, mix with the diced scallops and shelled prawns. Reduce the poaching liquid to 2 tablespoons, strain and mix with the dressing. Cook the potatoes unpeeled, until just tender, cool, peel and slice thickly. While still warm, cover with the dressing, leave to stand for 10 minutes, fold in the prepared shellfish and the chopped chives. Chill and divide between the four well-scrubbed deep scallop shells.

Celery in rich tomato

INGREDIENTS	METRIC	IMP.	U.S.
2 heads celery			
Canned whole tomatoes	*425 g*	*15 oz*	*2 cups*
2 tbspns tomato ketchup [catsup]			
1 medium onion, grated			
2 bay leaves			
Salt and pepper			
Butter			
Grated Cheddar cheese	*100 g*	*4 oz*	*1 cup*

Trim the tops and outer stalks from the celery and cut each head in half. Cook gently, covered, in boiling salted water until just tender. Meanwhile, clean and finely chop one or two outer stalks of celery. Cook with the canned tomatoes, tomato ketchup, onion and bay leaves for about 15 minutes, or until mixture is considerably reduced and thickened. Season to taste. Remove bay leaves. Butter a shallow ovenproof dish, place the well-drained celery halves in this, sprinkle with half the cheese, cover with the tomato mixture and sprinkle over remaining cheese. Place under a medium grill until cheese turns golden.

Gazpacho
Granada salad

Gazpacho

INGREDIENTS	METRIC	IMP.	U.S.
Ripe tomatoes	*750 g*	*$1\frac{1}{2}$ lb*	*$1\frac{1}{2}$ lb*
1 small onion			
1 small green pepper			
$\frac{1}{2}$ cucumber			
1 clove garlic			
6 tbspns oil			
3 tbspns white wine vinegar			
Chicken stock [broth]	*150 ml*	*$\frac{1}{4}$ pint*	*$\frac{1}{2}$ cup*
Tomato juice	*250 ml*	*8 fl oz*	*1 cup*
12 stuffed green olives			
Salt and freshly-ground black pepper			
Few drops Tabasco pepper sauce			
Chopped chives or parsley			

Skin the tomatoes, quarter them and remove the seeds. Chop the onion, deseed and chop the pepper, peel and dice the cucumber and crush the garlic. Place all these with the oil, vinegar, stock, tomato juice and olives in batches in a blender and liquidise until smooth. Season to taste with salt, pepper and Tabasco and chill for at least 30 minutes. Sprinkle with chives or parsley and serve with side dishes of more diced cucumber and green pepper, chopped tomato and onion, sliced stuffed olives and small fried bread croûtons.

Granada salad

INGREDIENTS	METRIC	IMP.	U.S.
OMELETTE			
2 eggs			
1 tbspn milk			
Pinch salt			
Few drops oil			
SALAD			
1 eating apple			
1 tbspn lemon juice			
1 small red pepper			
Button mushrooms	*100 g*	*4 oz*	*¼ lb*
1 lettuce			
Stuffed green olives	*75 g*	*3 oz*	*½ cup*
Cubed cooked potato	*225 g*	*8 oz*	*1 cup*
DRESSING			
2 tbspns olive oil			
2 tspns dry sherry			
2 tspns Worcestershire sauce			
1 tspn castor [granulated] sugar			
Salt and pepper			
1 tbspn chopped almonds			

Beat the eggs with the milk and salt to taste. Heat a little oil in an omelette pan, pour in the egg mixture and cook gently until set. Turn out of the pan and cool. Cut into squares. Core and slice the apple and toss with the lemon juice. Deseed the pepper and cut into strips, slice the mushrooms. Divide the lettuce into leaves and slice the olives. Arrange all the salad ingredients in a bowl with the omelette squares. Place all the ingredients for the dressing in a screw-topped jar and shake vigorously. Pour over the salad and toss just before serving.

Lobster mousse
Duck in vinegar jelly
Fresh tomato salad
Raspberries with yogurt

Lobster mousse

INGREDIENTS	METRIC	IMP.	U.S.
2 eggs			
Milk	*150 ml*	*$\frac{1}{4}$ pint*	*$\frac{1}{2}$ cup*
Fresh white breadcrumbs	*75 g*	*3 oz*	*$\frac{2}{3}$ cup*
Canned lobster or cooked lobster meat	*100 g* *100 g*	*$3\frac{3}{4}$ oz* *4 oz*	*$3\frac{3}{4}$ oz* *$\frac{1}{4}$ lb*
Cooked white fish	*100 g*	*4 oz*	*$\frac{1}{4}$ lb*
Melted butter	*25 g*	*1 oz*	*2 tbspns*
Salt and pepper			
Pinch dry mustard			
Few lettuce leaves			
Lemon halves			

Lightly beat the eggs and milk together, pour over the breadcrumbs and leave to soak for 10 minutes. Liquidise the lobster meat and flaked fish with the egg mixture, melted butter and seasonings. Pour into well-greased individual ovenproof dishes and place in a bain marie or a roasting tin, half-filled with boiling water, and bake in a moderately hot oven (375°F, 190°C, Gas Mark 5) for about 30 minutes, or until firm. Cool, loosen round the sides with a round-bladed knife and remove from the dishes. Serve chilled on lettuce leaves with lemon halves.

Duck in vinegar jelly

INGREDIENTS	METRIC	IMP.	U.S.
1 duck	*2 kg*	*$4\frac{1}{2}$ lb*	*$4\frac{1}{2}$ lb*
2 chicken stock [bouillon] cubes			
2 bay leaves			
2 cloves			
4 peppercorns			
1 egg white and shell			
Unflavoured gelatine [gelatin]	*15 g*	*$\frac{1}{2}$ oz*	*1 tbspn*
Vinegar	*6 tbspns*	*6 tbspns*	*$\frac{1}{2}$ cup*
Salt and pepper			
Thick mayonnaise	*150 ml*	*$\frac{1}{4}$ pint*	*$\frac{1}{2}$ cup*
Cucumber slices to garnish			

Cook the duck in a covered casserole in sufficient water to cover with the stock cubes, bay leaves and spices, for about 1 hour, until just tender. Remove the duck, cool, and drain the juices from it back into the casserole. Bone and cut the meat into large pieces. Reheat the stock, strain and make up to $1\frac{1}{4}$ pints/750 ml/3 cups with water if needed. Add the lightly beaten egg white and crushed shell and return to a clean saucepan. Boil until clear. Strain off the cleared stock and stir in the gelatine until dissolved. Add the vinegar, taste and adjust seasoning. Pour a little of the stock into the base of a shallow oval or rectangular mould. When set arrange a layer of duck on this, cover with stock and chill until firm. Add rest of duck meat, cover with remaining stock and chill. When set, loosen edges with a knife, dip base in hot water and turn out. Garnish with piped rosettes of mayonnaise and cucumber triangles. Serve with a fresh tomato salad.

Spanish herrings
Rabbit in vermouth with fennel
Blue cheese with apples

Spanish herrings

INGREDIENTS	METRIC	IMP.	U.S.
4 fresh herrings			
1 onion			
1 small root horseradish			
8 sliced stuffed green olives			
Sugar	*50 g*	*2 oz*	*$\frac{1}{4}$ cup*
4 tbspns water			
White wine vinegar	*200 ml*	*7 fl oz*	*$\frac{7}{8}$ cup*
2 tspns whole pickling spice			
2 bay leaves			

Have the herrings cleaned, boned and filleted. Thinly slice the onion into rings, scrub and shred the horseradish and slice the olives. Put the sugar, water and vinegar in a pan, heat gently until sugar dissolves, then boil for 2 minutes. Cool. Plunge the herring fillets in boiling water for about 3 seconds, drain and scrape off the skins with a knife. Layer the herrings in a shallow 2 pint/1 litre/5 cup dish with the remaining ingredients. Pour the vinegar over, cover and chill for 2-3 days, turning occasionally.

Rabbit in vermouth with fennel

INGREDIENTS	METRIC	IMP.	U.S.
4 small heads fennel			
1 young rabbit, jointed			
2 tbspns seasoned flour			
Butter	*75 g*	*3 oz*	*6 tbspns*
2 medium onions, chopped			
Dry vermouth	*100 ml*	*3 fl oz*	$\frac{1}{3}$ *cup*
1 bay leaf			
White stock	*300 ml*	$\frac{1}{2}$ *pint*	*1*$\frac{1}{4}$ *cups*
Salt and pepper			

Trim and halve the fennel. Remove and chop outer leaves. Turn the rabbit joints in the seasoned flour. Melt half the butter and use to fry the chopped onion and fennel leaves gently until limp. Add the rabbit joints and sauté, turning frequently, until golden brown on all sides. Add the vermouth, and allow to cook for 2 minutes, stirring constantly. Add the bay leaf and pour in the stock. Bring to the boil, reduce heat, cover and simmer for about 40 minutes, until the rabbit is tender. Meanwhile, turn the fennel halves in the remaining butter until well coated. Season to taste and add just enough water to cover. Cook over low heat, covered, for about 20 minutes, until tender. Remove lid and increase heat to make fennel halves golden on the outside. Serve with the rabbit.

A fruit and cheese platter makes the ideal course to end a meal and has the advantage that it can be prepared beforehand and kept lightly covered in a cool place. Most fruits, especially apples and pears, go well with cheese. If you offer more than one kind of cheese, choose a strongly flavoured hard variety, a mild flavoured one and a soft cheese. Keep wedges with cut surfaces wrapped in cling film until just before serving. Arrange the platter complete with cheese, fruit, butter dish with knife, and suitable knives for all the cheeses. If there is room put a small basket containing biscuits (crackers), crispbreads, wholemeal and crusty white bread on the platter. For non slimmers add a few nuts.

Swiss corn salad with tomato petals
Barbecued salmon steaks
Vegetable scallop

Swiss corn salad with tomato petals

INGREDIENTS	METRIC	IMP.	U.S.
3 tomatoes			
4 tbspns French [Italian] dressing			
1 large lettuce			
Cooked silverside [corned beef] or tongue	*100 g*	*4 oz*	*¼ lb*
Gruyère [Swiss] cheese	*100 g*	*4 oz*	*¼ lb*
Large bunch corn salad			

Halve the tomatoes, remove seeds and most of the flesh, divide each half into four. Press the flesh and seeds through a sieve and combine the tomato pulp with the dressing. Arrange beds of lettuce leaves in 4 individual salad dishes. Cut the meat and cheese into matchstick lengths. Toss the meat in the tomato dressing. Arrange sprigs of corn salad on the lettuce, divide the meat between the four dishes and top with the cheese sticks. Arrange tomato 'petals' decoratively around the salad.

Unusual salad greens make a change for slimmers who must eat a great deal of salad stuff. Look out for corn salad, chervil and endive. Young spinach leaves, carefully washed, also make good saladings. Try always to have plenty of fresh herbs on hand as various mixtures of chopped herbs can give lettuce new flavour excitement. Vary the dressings too, introducing fruit juices, or yogurt to give a mild, creamy texture without the addition of too many calories.

Barbecued salmon steaks

INGREDIENTS	METRIC	IMP.	U.S.
Dry white [Californian Chablis] wine	*100 ml*	*4 fl oz*	*½ cup*
¼ tspn dried marjoram			
1 tspn grated onion			
Pinch pepper			
4 salmon steaks			
Salt			

Combine the wine, marjoram, onion and pepper and pour over salmon steaks in a shallow dish. Refrigerate for several hours, turning the salmon once or twice. Drain well. Grill until the fish flakes easily with a fork, turning once. Sprinkle with salt as the salmon cooks.

Vegetable scallop

INGREDIENTS	METRIC	IMP.	U.S.
Runner [green] beans	*225 g*	*8 oz*	*½ lb*
Button onions	*225 g*	*8 oz*	*½ lb*
Sweetcorn kernels	*350 g*	*12 oz*	*¾ lb*
Butter	*25 g*	*1 oz*	*2 tbspns*
Milk	*150 ml*	*¼ pint*	*¾ cup*
1 tbspn cornflour [cornstarch]			
½ tspn prepared mustard			
½ tspn Worcestershire sauce			
½ tspn dried dill weed			
Natural [plain] yogurt	*150 ml*	*¼ pint*	*½ cup*
Salt and pepper			
Tomato wedges			

Cut the beans into short lengths. Cook with the onions and corn in a little boiling salted water until tender. Meanwhile, place the butter, milk and cornflour in a clean pan and bring to boiling point, whisking constantly. Add the mustard, Worcestershire sauce, dill, yogurt and seasoning to taste. Drain the vegetables and place in an ovenproof dish. Pour over the sauce, arrange tomato wedges on top and bake in a moderate oven (350°F, 180°C, Gas Mark 4) for about 15 minutes.

Chicken liver and olive ramekins
Lamb cutlets in aspic
Blackcurrant compôte with Slimmer's topping

Chicken liver and olive ramekins

INGREDIENTS	METRIC	IMP.	U.S.
1 medium onion			
1 clove garlic			
Butter	*100 g*	*4 oz*	*¼ lb*
Chicken livers	*175 g*	*6 oz*	*6 oz*
1 tbspn chopped mixed herbs or 1 tspn dried mixed herbs			
1 tbspn brandy			
Salt and pepper			
6 stuffed green olives			

Chop the onion and crush the garlic. Cook in 25 g/1 oz/2 tablespoons of the butter until soft. Add the livers and cook for 3 minutes. Stir in the herbs. Melt a further 50 g/2 oz/4 tablespoons of the butter. Liquidise the liver mixture in a blender with the brandy and melted butter until smooth. Season to taste. Divide between 3 ramekin dishes and chill until firm. Melt the remaining butter and spoon over the pâté. When set, decorate with sliced olives. Serves 3.

Lamb cutlets in aspic

INGREDIENTS	METRIC	IMP.	U.S.
6 small lamb cutlets			
Salt and black pepper			
Melted butter	*50 g*	*2 oz*	*$\frac{1}{4}$ cup*
Liquid aspic jelly	*300 ml*	*$\frac{1}{2}$ pint*	*$1\frac{1}{4}$ cups*
1 tbspn dry sherry			
6 mint leaves			
1 lemon			
Few lettuce leaves			
1 cooked carrot, sliced			

Season the cutlets with salt and black pepper. Brush with melted butter and cook under a hot grill for 3 minutes on each side. Cool. Make up the aspic jelly and stir in the sherry. Allow to cool and become syrupy. Place 1 mint leaf on each cutlet and coat several times with aspic jelly to build up a shiny glaze. Cover cutlet bones with paper frills. Thinly slice the lemon and arrange a bed of lettuce leaves on a serving dish. Place each cutlet on a circle of lemon topped with a carrot slice. Serve very cold. Serves 3.

Blackcurrant Compôte can be made by topping and tailing 12 oz/350 g/2 cups blackcurrants and stewing with 8 tablespoons of orange juice until soft. Add liquid sweetener to taste.

Slimmer's topping Dissolve 1 teaspoon gelatine (gelatin) in 2 tablespoons water in a basin over a pan of hot water. Stir in 4 tablespoons dry skimmed milk powder, 125 ml/4 fl oz/$\frac{1}{2}$ cup cold water, $\frac{1}{2}$ teaspoon lemon juice, $\frac{1}{2}$ teaspoon vanilla essence (extract) and a few drops of liquid artificial sweetener. Whisk with an electric mixer until the mixture thickens and will just hold its shape. Serve with the blackcurrant compôte.

Crab imperial
Steak with apple rice

Crab imperial

INGREDIENTS	METRIC	IMP.	U.S.
1 green pepper			
Butter	*15 g*	*½ oz*	*1 tbspn*
1 canned red pimiento			
3 tbspns mayonnaise			
1 tspn Worcestershire sauce			
1 tspn salt			
¼ tspn dry mustard			
Crab meat	*450 g*	*1 lb*	*1 lb*
1 tbspn dry sherry			
Grated Cheddar cheese	*25 g*	*1 oz*	*¼ cup*
½ tspn paprika pepper			

Chop the green pepper finely. Sauté in the butter for 2 minutes. Cool. Chop the canned pimiento finely. Stir the green pepper, pimiento, mayonnaise, Worcestershire sauce, salt, and dry mustard into the crab meat, mixing thoroughly. Spoon the mixture into cleaned crab shells or a baking dish. Sprinkle the sherry, cheese and paprika over the crab mixture. Bake in a moderate oven (350°F, 180°C, Gas Mark 4) for 20 minutes or until heated through.

Steak with apple rice

INGREDIENTS	METRIC	IMP.	U.S.
Water	*600 ml*	*1 pint*	*2½ cups*
Salt			
Strip of lemon rind			
1 tspn oil			
1 tbspn sugar			
Long grain rice	*225 g*	*8 oz*	*½ lb*
Eating apples	*450 g*	*1 lb*	*1 lb*
Pinch ground cinnamon			
4 rump steaks or 8 frozen steaklets			
Butter	*25 g*	*1 oz*	*2 tbspns*

Bring the water, salt, lemon rind, oil and sugar to the boil. Add the rice and peeled, cored and sliced apples. Season with cinnamon. Stir, lower heat to simmer, cover and cook for 15 minutes, or until the rice and apples are tender and the liquid absorbed. Fry the steaks or steaklets in the butter and serve on a bed of apple rice.

Pineapple juice cocktail
Sausages with French beans
and bacon rice

Sausages with French beans and bacon rice

INGREDIENTS	METRIC	IMP.	U.S.
Long grain rice	*225 g*	*8 oz*	*1 cup*
Water	*600 ml*	*1 pint*	*$2\frac{1}{2}$ cups*
Salt and pepper			
Sausages [pork links] with herbs	*750 g*	*$1\frac{1}{2}$ lb*	*$1\frac{1}{2}$ lb*
French beans	*750 g*	*$1\frac{1}{2}$ lb*	*$1\frac{1}{2}$ lb*
1 large onion			
Oil for frying			
Bacon	*75 g*	*3 oz*	*3 slices*
2 tbspns chopped parsley			

Place the rice, water and 1 teaspoon salt in a saucepan. Bring to boiling point, stir once, cover and simmer for about 15 minutes, until the rice is cooked and the liquid absorbed. Prick the sausages with a fork, and cook under a hot grill (broiler) for about 15 minutes, until golden brown all over. Cook the beans in boiling salted water until tender but still firm. Drain well. Thinly slice the onion and fry in 2 tablespoons oil for 4 minutes. Stir in the beans, season with a little pepper, cover and cook gently for 10 minutes. Chop the bacon and fry in 1 teaspoon oil until golden. Combine the rice, parsley and bacon and spoon into a serving dish. Arrange the sausages and bean mixture on another dish.

Navarin printanier
Spinach noodle cake

Navarin printanier

INGREDIENTS	METRIC	IMP.	U.S.
2 tbspns oil			
8 small lamb chops or cutlets			
1 medium onion, sliced			
8 young carrots, sliced			
1 stalk celery, sliced			
12 button onions			
Flour	*25 g*	*1 oz*	$\frac{1}{4}$ *cup*
Stock [broth]	*450 ml*	$\frac{3}{4}$ *pint*	$1\frac{3}{4}$ *cups*
Few drops gravy browning			
Bouquet garni			
Salt and pepper			
Canned red pimientoes	*70 g*	$2\frac{3}{4}$ *oz*	$2\frac{3}{4}$ *oz*
2 eating apples			
1 tbspn chopped parsley			

Heat the oil and use to sauté the lamb chops until browned. Remove meat and add all the vegetables except the pimiento. Cook for about 4 minutes, stirring. Stir in the flour and gradually add the stock. Bring to the boil, stirring constantly and add the gravy browning, bouquet garni and seasoning. Chop the pimiento roughly and add to the stew with the liquid from the can. Replace the meat and simmer for 20 minutes. Core and slice the apple, add to the pan and cook for a further 5 minutes. Discard the bouquet garni, adjust the seasoning and serve hot garnished with chopped parsley.

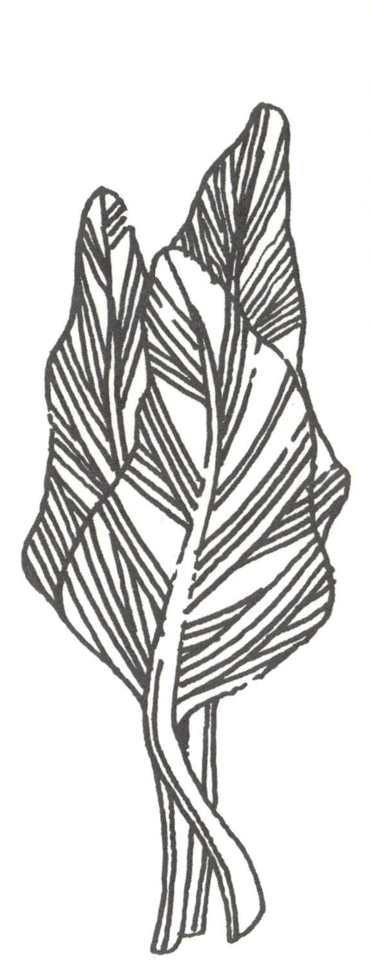

Spinach noodle cake

INGREDIENTS	METRIC	IMP.	U.S.
Spinach	*1 kg*	*2 lb*	*2 lb*
Noodles	*225 g*	*8 oz*	*½ lb*
Butter	*25 g*	*1 oz*	*2 tbspns*
Grated cheese	*175 g*	*6 oz*	*1½ cups*
3 eggs			
Milk	*450 ml*	*¾ pint*	*2 cups –*
½ tspn ground mace			
Salt and black pepper			

Wash and cook the spinach in just sufficient boiling salted water to prevent it from burning, drain and chop finely. Cook the noodles in plenty of boiling salted water for 8 minutes, or until just tender but not soft. Drain well, and toss in half the butter. Grease an ovenproof dish with remaining butter, put a layer of spinach in the bottom, sprinkle in half the cheese, then add the noodles, a little more cheese, the remaining spinach and the rest of the cheese. Beat the eggs, milk and mace, add seasoning and pour over the dish. Bake in a moderate oven (350°F, 180°C, Gas Mark 4) for 30-40 minutes.

Minced meat rolls with Palma salad
Leek and bacon bake
Fresh orange dessert

Minced meat rolls with Palma salad

INGREDIENTS	METRIC	IMP.	U.S.
2 large mild onions			
Cooked long grain rice	*150 g*	*6 oz*	*1½ cups*
Minced [ground] beef	*225 g*	*8 oz*	*½ lb*
1 tbspn capers			
Salt and pepper			
1 tspn made mustard			
½ tspn grated lemon rind			
1 egg, beaten			
3 tbspns corn oil			
2 medium tomatoes			
1 tspn wine vinegar			
Paprika pepper			
Celery salt			

Chop one of the onions finely and mix with the rice and minced beef, then blend in the capers, seasonings, mustard and lemon rind. Bind the mixture with beaten egg and form into long rolls with floured hands. Fry the rolls in 2 tablespoons of the oil until crisp and browned on all sides. Meanwhile slice the tomatoes and remaining onion finely, season with salt. Mix together the remaining oil and the vinegar with paprika and celery salt to taste. Pour over the tomatoes. Toss with the onion rings. Serve the salad with the hot meat rolls.

Leek and bacon bake

INGREDIENTS	METRIC	IMP.	U.S.
8 medium leeks			
8 slices streaky [side] bacon			
Grated Lancashire [American] cheese	*100 g*	*4 oz*	*1 cup*

Trim the leeks to an even length and cut in half lengthwise. Wash well. Derind and snip up the bacon. Cook the leeks in boiling salted water, covered, until tender. Drain well. Meanwhile, fry the bacon in a heavy-based pan without added fat until golden. Use the rendered fat to grease a shallow flameproof dish. Sprinkle in a little of the grated cheese, cover with a layer of leeks, sprinkle over some of the bacon and repeat with remaining ingredients, ending with a layer of cheese. Pour over the rest of the rendered bacon fat and place under a hot grill until the cheese melts and is bubbling.

Fresh fruit desserts need no cooking but sometimes look more attractive than the same fruit served in a bowl or basket. To make a fresh orange dessert, peel and slice the fruit, allowing one orange per person. Arrange the rings overlapping on small plates and sprinkle with toasted flaked almonds and toasted coconut. To make a grapefruit dessert, halve the grapefruits, remove the pips, spoon out the flesh and scrape out all the pith. Return the flesh to the empty cups and sprinkle with a little peppermint flavoured syrup and chopped mint leaves.

Tongue and asparagus custard
Broad bean salad

Tongue and asparagus custard

INGREDIENTS	METRIC	IMP.	U.S.
Milk	*450 ml*	*¾ pint*	*2 cups*
4 eggs			
1 tspn salt			
Freshly ground black pepper			
½ tspn celery seed			
½ tspn dried dill weed (optional)			
Cooked asparagus spears	*450 g*	*1 lb*	*1 lb*
Canned ox tongue	*100 g*	*4 oz*	*4 oz*

Beat the milk, eggs, seasoning and herbs together. Reserve 6 asparagus spears for garnish. Chop the remainder and the tongue and add to the custard mixture. Pour into a well greased flan dish and bake in a moderately hot oven (375°F, 190°C, Gas Mark 5) for 35 minutes. Serve hot garnished with the reserved asparagus spears.

Broad bean salad

INGREDIENTS	METRIC	IMP.	U.S.
New potatoes	*225 g*	*8 oz*	*½ lb*
4 tbspns French [Italian] dressing			
Plain yogurt	*150 ml*	*¼ pint*	*½ cup+*
1 tbspn chopped fresh dill or 1 tspn dill weed			
4 spring onions [scallions], chopped			
Salt and pepper			
Broad beans, shelled	*450 g*	*1 lb*	*1 lb*

Scrub the potatoes and cook in boiling salted water until just tender. Drain and peel. Cut them into halves or quarters according to size. Beat the French dressing into the yogurt, stir in the chopped dill and the spring onion and adjust seasoning to taste. Fold in the potatoes and raw beans and chill for at least 1 hour.

Nettle and spinach soup
Haddock with tomato topping

Nettle and spinach soup

INGREDIENTS	METRIC	IMP.	U.S.
Young nettle leaves	*450 g*	*1 lb*	*1 lb*
Spinach	*450 g*	*1 lb*	*1 lb*
1 chicken stock [bouillon] cube			
Water	*600 ml*	*1 pint*	*2½ cups*
Butter	*25 g*	*1 oz*	*2 tbspns*
Plain [all-purpose] flour	*25 g*	*1 oz*	*¼ cup*
Salt and pepper			
Pinch ground nutmeg			
3 tbspns plain yogurt			

Pour boiling water over the nettle leaves and spinach. Drain thoroughly and chop coarsely. Dissolve the stock cube in the water and simmer the chopped nettle leaves and spinach in the stock for 30 minutes. Sieve or liquidise in a blender, return to the saucepan and stir in the butter kneaded with the flour. Bring to the boil and simmer for 5 minutes. Season to taste with salt and pepper and add the nutmeg. Swirl the yogurt through the soup just before serving.

Haddock with tomato topping

INGREDIENTS	METRIC	IMP.	U.S.
Onions	*450 g*	*1 lb*	*1 lb*
3 tbspns oil			
Mushrooms	*225 g*	*8 oz*	*½ lb*
Salt and pepper			
1 tspn dried thyme			
1 tspn dried savory			
Fillet fresh haddock	*675 g*	*1½ lb*	*1½ lb*
6 small tomatoes			
White wine	*50 ml*	*2 fl oz*	*¼ cup*
Gruyère cheese, grated	*50 g*	*2 oz*	*½ cup*

Cut the onions in very fine slices. Sauté in the oil until golden brown. When the onion is soft, add the sliced mushrooms and seasoning. Stir gently until the mushrooms begin to render their juice. Turn half the contents of the pan into a buttered ovenproof dish, sprinkle with some of the herbs. Arrange the fish on top, season and cover with the remaining onion mixture then with the quartered tomatoes. Pour over the wine, sprinkle with the rest of the herbs and the grated cheese. Place in a moderate oven (350°F, 180°C, Gas Mark 4) for 35 minutes.

Salmon shell salad
Stuffed cabbage rolls
Sherried onion rings

Salmon shell salad

INGREDIENTS	METRIC	IMP.	U.S.
Small pasta shells	*100 g*	*4 oz*	*1 cup*
Cooked fresh or canned salmon	*350 g*	*12 oz*	*¾ lb*
Length of cucumber	*10 cm*	*4 inch*	*4 inch*
Soured cream	*150 ml*	*¼ pint*	*½ cup +*
Salt and ground black pepper			
Cress and lemon slices to garnish			

Cook the pasta shells in boiling salted water for 7 minutes, or until just tender. Drain well. Meanwhile, break up the salmon, removing any skin and bones. Chop the unpeeled cucumber and mix carefully with the fish and pasta. Season the cream with salt and pepper and stir gently into the fish mixture. Adjust the seasoning and divide the mixture between 4 scallop shells or individual dishes. Garnish with cress and lemon slices cut into the shape of butterflies. Serve with thin slices of brown bread and butter.

Piped potato rosettes add a professional finish to many dishes, yet they are so easy to make. Prepare some instant mashed potato using half milk and half water. Beat in an egg yolk and plenty of seasoning, including a pinch of nutmeg. Pipe out, using a large rose nozzle (pipe), in place on the dish, or on a greased baking sheet. If liked, the sheet can be placed in the oven to colour the rosettes. Remove and put in place using a spatula while still hot.

Sherried onion rings

INGREDIENTS	METRIC	IMP.	U.S.
3 medium onions			
½ tspn salt			
¼ tspn freshly ground black pepper			
Butter	*50 g*	*2 oz*	*¼ cup*
Dry sherry	*50 ml*	*2 fl oz*	*¼ cup*
2 tbspns flaked [slivered] almonds			

Slice the onions and separate them into rings. Season with salt and pepper. Melt the butter in a large frying pan. Toss the onion rings in the melted butter. Cook until tender, but not browned. Add the sherry and cook for a further 2-3 minutes, then stir in the flaked almonds.

Stuffed cabbage rolls

INGREDIENTS	METRIC	IMP.	U.S.
4 large leaves Savoy cabbage			
Butter	*40 g*	*1½ oz*	*3 tbspns*
Minced [ground] beef	*225 g*	*8 oz*	*½ lb*
1 small onion, chopped			
Salt and pepper			
Fresh white breadcrumbs	*175 g*	*6 oz*	*2 cups*
Good pinch grated nutmeg			
½ tspn dried marjoram			
Grated Parmesan cheese	*25 g*	*1 oz*	*¼ cup*
1 egg			
2 tbspns oil			
1 beef stock [bouillon] cube			
Water	*300 ml*	*½ pint*	*1¼ cups*
Mashed potato	*225 g*	*8 oz*	*2 cups*

Trim the hard stems from the base of the cabbage leaves and blanch in boiling salted water for about 10 minutes, or until tender. Melt ½ oz/15 g of the butter and use to sauté the beef and onion until lightly browned. Season with salt and pepper. Combine with the breadcrumbs, nutmeg, marjoram, Parmesan and the lightly beaten egg. Divide the stuffing between the cabbage leaves and roll each up into a parcel. Tie a piece of thread round the centre of each parcel, following the spine of the leaf. Brown the rolls on all sides in the remaining butter and the oil in a shallow flameproof dish. Dissolve the stock cube in the water, pour over, and braise, covered, for 45 minutes, over low heat. Remove the thread, place the rolls on a serving dish, reduce remaining stock to a few spoonfuls and pour over the rolls. Serve garnished with piped rosettes of mashed potato.

Egg petal soup
Cartwheel salad
Mushroom rolls

Egg petal soup

INGREDIENTS	METRIC	IMP.	U.S.
Raw chicken breast meat	*100 g*	*4 oz*	*$\frac{1}{4}$ lb*
1 tspn dry sherry			
1 tspn soy sauce			
1 tspn cornflour [cornstarch]			
2 tbspns cooking oil			
Chicken stock [broth]	*900 ml*	*$1\frac{1}{2}$ pints*	*4 cups*
1 spring onion [scallion] sliced			
Salt and pepper			
1 egg			

Slice the chicken breast meat into julienne strips. Mix the sherry, soy sauce and cornflour with the chicken strips. Heat the oil in a frying pan and quickly fry the chicken strips until nicely browned, about 2 minutes. Bring the chicken stock to the boil and add the fried chicken strips, sliced onion, salt and pepper. Simmer for 10 minutes. Beat the egg lightly and stir into the soup. Remove from the heat and serve immediately.

Cartwheel salad

INGREDIENTS	METRIC	IMP.	U.S.
Lettuce leaves			
1 cucumber			
Canned sweetcorn niblets	*210 g*	*$7\frac{1}{2}$ oz*	*$7\frac{1}{2}$ oz*
12 large grapes			
Cottage cheese	*100 g*	*4 oz*	*$\frac{2}{3}$ cup*
Diced cooked ham	*50 g*	*2 oz*	*$\frac{1}{3}$ cup*
Drained canned pineapple pieces	*50 g*	*2 oz*	*$\frac{1}{3}$ cup*
DRESSING			
Natural [plain] yogurt	*150 ml*	*$\frac{1}{4}$ pint*	*$\frac{1}{2}$ cup*
2 tbspns syrup from canned pineapple			
Salt and pepper			
2 tbspns chopped chives			

Arrange a bed of lettuce leaves on a round serving plate. Slice the cucumber and with the slices as spokes, make a cartwheel shape with 8 divisions on top of the lettuce. Fill 4 divisions with sweetcorn niblets. Halve and pip the grapes. Reserve 6 halves and combine the remainder with the cottage cheese. Place in 2 sections of the 'wheel'. Fill the remaining 2 sections with diced ham and pineapple pieces. Arrange more cucumber slices round the edge of the plate. To make the dressing, beat together the yogurt, pineapple syrup and seasoning to taste. Stir in the chives and serve in a sauceboat with the salad.

Mushroom rolls

INGREDIENTS	METRIC	IMP.	U.S.
12 thin slices white bread			
Mushrooms	*225 g*	*8 oz*	*½ lb*
Butter	*50 g*	*1 oz*	*2 tbspns*
1 tspn grated [minced] onion			
1 tbspn lemon juice			
½ tspn curry powder			
Pinch cayenne			
Salt and pepper			
Melted butter			
Chopped parsley			

Remove the crusts from the bread and roll the slices with a rolling pin to flatten. Chop the mushrooms very finely and sauté in the butter until tender. Stir in the onion, lemon juice, curry powder and cayenne. Cook for 2-3 minutes. Season to taste with salt and pepper. Spread the mushroom mixture thinly on each bread slice. Roll up and fasten the ends with wooden cocktail sticks. Place the rolls on a lightly greased baking sheet and brush each roll with melted butter. Bake in a moderately hot oven (400°F, 200°C, Gas Mark 6) for 15 minutes or until nicely browned. Serve hot, garnished with chopped parsley.

Carrot and sweet pepper soup
Perfection piperade

Carrot and sweet pepper soup

INGREDIENTS	METRIC	IMP.	U.S.
1 red pepper			
Carrots	*450 g*	*1 lb*	*1 lb*
Onions	*225 g*	*8 oz*	*$\frac{1}{2}$ lb*
2 stalks celery			
Butter	*50 g*	*2 oz*	*$\frac{1}{4}$ cup*
Chicken stock [broth]	*1 litre*	*$1\frac{3}{4}$ pints*	*$4\frac{1}{4}$ cups*
Salt and pepper			
Single cream [half & half]	*150 ml*	*$\frac{1}{4}$ pint*	*$\frac{1}{2}$ cup*

Deseed the pepper, cut a few strips for the decoration and roughly chop the remainder. Chop the carrots, onions and celery. Place all these in a pan with the butter and fry gently until soft. Add the stock, bring to boiling point, cover and simmer for 45 minutes. Season well, cool and liquidize in a blender until smooth. Reheat and stir in the cream. Meanwhile, blanch the pepper strips in boiling salted water for 1 minute, then drain. Serve the soup in a hot serving bowl and garnish with the pepper strips.

Perfection piperade

INGREDIENTS	METRIC	IMP.	U.S.
2 rashers [slices] bacon			
1 medium green pepper			
1 medium red pepper			
1 large onion			
6 inner stalks celery			
Butter	*50 g*	*2 oz*	*$\frac{1}{4}$ cup*
$\frac{1}{2}$ tspn dried mixed herbs			
Salt and pepper			
4 eggs			
Paprika pepper			

Cut the bacon into strips. Deseed and slice the peppers. Slice the onion and celery. Simmer the pepper slices and celery in just sufficient salted water to cover for 5 minutes, or until almost tender. Drain well. Meanwhile, melt the butter in a deep frying pan, add the bacon, onion, herbs and seasoning to taste. Cover and cook gently for 5 minutes, or until the onion is soft. Add the pepper and celery, stir well and cover. Cook gently for a further 10 minutes or until all the vegetables are soft. Make 4 hollows in the mixture with the back of a spoon and break one egg into each. Cover and continue cooking gently until the eggs are set. Sprinkle with a little paprika pepper before serving.

Wholewheat cob loaf with Watercress soup or Wholewheat flower pot loaves with Lettuce and parsley soup

Wholewheat bread

INGREDIENTS	METRIC	IMP.	U.S.
3 tbspns dried yeast or fresh [compressed] yeast	*25 g*	*1 oz*	*1 cake*
Warm water	*300 ml*	*½ pint*	*1¼ cups*
Milk	*450 ml*	*¾ pint*	*2 cups*
Margarine	*50 g*	*2 oz*	*¼ cup*
Treacle [molasses]	*125 ml*	*4 fl oz*	*½ cup*
1 tbspn salt			
Wholewheat flour	*1 kg*	*2 lb*	*8 cups*
2 tbspns wheat germ			

Dissolve the yeast in the warm water and set in a warm place until frothy. Scald the milk; add the margarine, treacle, and salt. Cool to lukewarm. Beat in 8 oz/225 g flour and the wheat germ. Beat for two minutes. Stir in the yeast liquid and sufficient flour to make a stiff dough. Turn out on a lightly floured board and knead until the dough is smooth and elastic, about 10 minutes. Place in a greased bowl, cover with a damp cloth and let rise until doubled in bulk, about 1 hour.

Round cob

Shape one half of the dough into a round and place on a greased baking sheet. Cover and let rise in a warm place until almost doubled. Bake in a moderately hot oven (400°F, 200°C, Gas Mark 6) for 10 minutes, then lower heat to moderate (350°F, 180°C, Gas Mark 4) for 30 minutes. Allow loaf to cool on a wire rack.

Flower-pot loaves

Shape the remainder of the dough into three balls. Place each ball in a well greased earthenware pot measuring 5 inches/13 cm diameter at the top. Brush the top of the dough with salt and water and sprinkle with cracked wheat. Cover and let rise in a warm place until the dough reaches the top of the pots. Bake in a hot oven (425°F, 220°C, Gas Mark 7) for 30 minutes.

Watercress soup

INGREDIENTS	METRIC	IMP.	U.S.
1 stalk celery			
6 small white onions			
1 clove garlic			
2 tbspns oil			
1 tspn dried thyme			
1 bay leaf			
1 bunch watercress			
1 tbspn flour			
2 chicken stock [bouillon] cubes			
Boiling water	*900 ml*	*1½ pints*	*4 cups—*

Chop the celery and a little of the leaves, quarter the onions and crush the garlic. Cook the vegetables gently in the oil until limp but not coloured. Add the thyme and bay leaf. Chop the watercress roughly, add to the pan, sprinkle on the flour and stir well. Gradually add the stock cubes dissolved in the water and bring to the boil, stirring constantly. Simmer for 20 minutes and serve at once hot. Or, serve chilled, garnished with single cream.

Lettuce and parsley soup

INGREDIENTS	METRIC	IMP.	U.S.
Butter	*40 g*	*$1\frac{1}{2}$ oz*	*3 tbspns*
2 large lettuces			
2 medium onions			
2 cloves garlic			
Water	*600 ml*	*1 pint*	*$2\frac{1}{2}$ cups*
Salt and pepper			
2 slices bread			
4 tbspns chopped parsley			
2 tbspns chopped chervil			
Double [whipping] cream	*4 tbspns*	*4 tbspns*	*$\frac{1}{3}$ cup*

Melt the butter in a large saucepan. Carefully wash the lettuce leaves and add a few at a time to the butter. Chop the onions finely, crush the garlic and add both to the pan. Cover the contents with the water and bring to the boil. Season to taste, cover and simmer for 20 minutes. Remove the crusts from the bread and add bread to the soup. Liquidise or sieve the soup and reheat to boiling point. Pour into a tureen and stir in the herbs and the cream just before serving.

Three bean soup
Carrot loaf with ham platter

Three bean soup

INGREDIENTS	METRIC	IMP.	U.S.
White haricot [navy] beans	*225 g*	*8 oz*	$\frac{1}{2}$ *lb*
Red kidney beans	*225 g*	*8 oz*	$\frac{1}{2}$ *lb*
French [green] beans	*225 g*	*8 oz*	$\frac{1}{2}$ *lb*
1 large onion			
1 clove garlic			
Tomatoes	*225 g*	*8 oz*	$\frac{1}{2}$ *lb*
1 small red sweet pepper			
2 tbspns oil			
2 medium potatoes, diced			
Salt and pepper			
2 tbspns chopped basil			

Soak the dried beans overnight in cold water, then drain. Trim and halve the French beans. Finely chop the onion, crush the garlic, peel and chop the tomatoes and deseed and chop the pepper. Heat the oil, use to fry, pepper, onion and garlic until softened. Reserve 2 tablespoons of chopped tomato and add the remainder to the pan with the beans, potato and water to cover. Season and bring to the boil. Cover and simmer for about 45 minutes, until the beans are tender. Add the herbs and reserved tomato and cook for a further 10 minutes. Serves 8.

Carrot loaf

INGREDIENTS	METRIC	IMP.	U.S.
Carrots	*2 kg*	*4 lb*	*4 lb*
1 medium onion, grated			
3 tbspns fine semolina			
2 tspns flour			
6 eggs			
4 tbspns single cream [half & half]			
Salt and pepper			
½ tspn grated nutmeg			
Watercress to garnish			

Slice the carrots and cook in boiling salted water until tender, then liquidise or purée and mix with the onion. Beat in the semolina, flour, lightly beaten eggs, cream, salt, pepper and nutmeg. Pour the mixture into a well greased 2 lb/1 kg loaf tin and bake in a moderate oven (350°F, 180°C, Gas Mark 4) for 1 hour. Turn out onto a clean kitchen towel, cover with a warm serving dish and turn over. Serve sliced, garnished with watercress. Serves 8.

Note: **This loaf is particularly good served with hot sliced gammon or cold ham.**

Courgette soup
Haddock with pink prawn sauce
Fresh fruit melon compôte

Courgette soup

INGREDIENTS	METRIC	IMP.	U.S.
1 clove garlic			
1 onion			
Courgettes [zucchini]	*1 kg*	*2 lb*	*2 lb*
1 tbspn olive oil			
Beef stock [broth]	*1.5 litres*	*3 pints*	*7½ cups*
½ tspn dried thyme			
½ tspn dried sage			
Long grain rice	*75 g*	*3 oz*	*½ cup*
Pepper			
4 tbspns grated Parmesan cheese			

Crush the garlic, chop the onion and slice the courgettes. Heat the oil in a saucepan and use to fry the garlic and onion until soft. Add the stock, bring to the boil and add the courgettes, thyme and sage. Sprinkle in the rice. Stir carefully and simmer for 15-20 minutes. Season the soup with the pepper and serve with grated Parmesan cheese sprinkled on top. Serves 6.

Haddock with pink prawn sauce

INGREDIENTS	METRIC	IMP.	U.S.
2 large haddock fillets			
1 lemon			
Salt and ground black pepper			
SAUCE			
Butter	*25 g*	*1 oz*	*2 tbspns*
Flour	*25 g*	*1 oz*	*¼ cup*
Milk	*300 ml*	*½ pint*	*1¼ cups*
1 tspn salt			
Black pepper to taste			
2 tspns tomato purée [paste]			
2 tspns paprika pepper			
Canned prawns [shrimp]	*396 g*	*14 oz*	*2 cups*

Rinse and skin the haddock and dry on absorbent kitchen paper. Put the fillets into an ovenproof dish. Grate the rind from the lemon and squeeze the juice. Spoon rind and juice over the fish, and sprinkle with salt and pepper. Cover and bake in a moderate oven (350°F, 180°C, Gas Mark 4) for 20 minutes. Lift fillets on to serving dish and keep warm. To make the sauce, melt the butter in a saucepan, stir in the flour and cook for 1 minute without allowing it to colour. Gradually add the milk, seasoning, tomato purée, and paprika and bring to the boil, stirring constantly. Add any juices left from cooking the fish. Cook gently for 2 minutes. Meanwhile pound the prawns until smooth, stir into the sauce and adjust seasoning. Serve the fish with the sauce spooned over. Serves 6.

Fresh fruit melon compôte

INGREDIENTS	METRIC	IMP.	U.S.
Grape juice	*150 ml*	*¼ pint*	*½ cup*
Orange marmalade	*50 g*	*2 oz*	*¼ cup*
2 tbspns sweet white wine			
1 large honeydew melon			
½ cantaloupe			
Green grapes	*100 g*	*4 oz*	*1 cup*
Strawberries	*225 g*	*8 oz*	*½ lb*

Combine the grape juice, orange marmalade and sweet white wine. Cut the top off the honeydew melon and remove the seeds. Scoop out the pulp with a melon ball cutter. Dice the pulp from the cantaloupe. Peel and remove the seeds from the grapes. Slice the strawberries in half. Mix the prepared fruits with the grape juice liquid. Spoon into the honeydew melon shell. Chill thoroughly before serving. Serves 6.

Grilled grapefruit with brown sugar
Mushroom stuffed peppers
Fluffy boiled rice with chopped parsley
Strawberry sorbet

Grilled grapefruit with brown sugar

INGREDIENTS	METRIC	IMP.	U.S.
2 pink grapefruit			
4 tbspns soft [light] brown sugar			
1 tbspn rum			

Cut the grapefruit in half and remove white pith from centres. Loosen segments if necessary. Mix the sugar with the rum, fill centres and spread partly over the surface of the cut halves. Place under a moderately hot grill for a few minutes until sugar melts and caramelises. Serve hot.

Stuffed vegetables are good for slimmers because a well-flavoured savoury stuffing enhances but makes only a small part of the main dish. The vegetable 'cups' are usually low in calorie value. Other vegetables which could be used with the stuffing given opposite are blanched marrow rings, large scooped-out tomatoes, parboiled onions also scooped out, and aubergines (egg plants) sliced lengthwise. Cooked rice can be used as an alternative to soft white breadcrumbs, or lightly cooked small pasta shapes.

Mushroom stuffed peppers

INGREDIENTS	METRIC	IMP.	U.S.
4 medium green peppers			
Button mushrooms	*100 g*	*4 oz*	*1 cup*
1 slice lean bacon			
Butter	*25 g*	*1 oz*	*2 tbspns*
1 small onion, chopped			
4 chicken livers			
1 tbspn soft white breadcrumbs			
SAUCE			
Ripe tomatoes	*350 g*	*12 oz*	*¾ lb*
1 tspn sugar			
Salt and pepper			
Few drops Tabasco pepper sauce			

Remove the stem ends from the peppers and scoop out the seeds. Pour boiling water over the pepper 'cases' to blanch them, leave 2-3 minutes, then drain well. Slice the mushrooms, reserving 4 for the garnish, derind and chop the bacon. Cook the chopped bacon in a frying pan over moderate heat until the fat runs, add the butter, onion, mushrooms and chicken livers. Cook until livers are just firm. Remove the 4 whole mushrooms and keep warm. Remove and chop the livers finely. Return to the pan with the breadcrumbs and stir until the breadcrumbs begin to turn colour. Divide the filling between the 4 pepper cases, and arrange upright in an ovenproof baking dish. To make the sauce, chop the tomatoes and place in a pan with the sugar, seasoning and Tabasco. Cook over moderate heat until thickened, about 10 minutes. Sieve and pour round the peppers in the dish. Spoon a little tomato mixture over the stuffing, cover with foil and bake in a moderate oven (350°F, 180°C, Gas Mark 4) for 35 minutes. Uncover and garnish with the reserved mushrooms.

Strawberry sorbet

INGREDIENTS	METRIC	IMP.	U.S.
Sweetened strawberry purée	*450 ml*	*¾ pint*	*2 cups –*
2 tbspns lemon juice			
4 tbspns orange juice			

Blend the purée with the fruit juices and pour into a shallow container. Cover with freezer film and freeze until ice crystals begin to form. Remove from the freezer, beat thoroughly, return to the container and freeze until firm. (The consistency will be more like that of an Italian 'Granita', but is very pleasant.)

Polish beetroot salad
Rabbit with game sauce
Melon balls in wine

Polish beetroot salad

INGREDIENTS	METRIC	IMP.	U.S.
Slice cooked tongue	*100 g*	*4 oz*	$\frac{1}{4}$ *lb*
1 large cooked beetroot [beet]			
4 fillets salt herring			
4 tbspns French [Italian] dressing			
1 hard-boiled egg			
1 tbspn chopped parsley			

Roughly chop the tongue, dice the beetroot and quarter the herring fillets. Toss the beetroot, herring and tongue in the salad dressing. Reserve four centre slices of the egg for garnish, chop the rest roughly and put in the bottom of a salad bowl. Cover with half the tossed ingredients and sprinkle with a little parsley. Fill up the bowl with the remaining ingredients, garnish with the reserved egg slices and the rest of the parsley.

Rabbit with game sauce

INGREDIENTS	METRIC	IMP.	U.S.
1 young rabbit			
2 tbspns flour			
1 tspn salt			
3 tbspns oil			
Button onions	*175 g*	*6 oz*	*6 oz*
Canned game soup	*425 g*	*15 oz*	*15 oz*
Stock	*300 ml*	*$\frac{1}{2}$ pint*	*$1\frac{1}{4}$ cups*
1 bay leaf			
Salt and pepper			
2 tspns cornflour [cornstarch]			
Canned flageolets [lima beans]	*425 g*	*15 oz*	*15 oz*

Joint the rabbit and coat the joints in the flour mixed with the salt. Fry in one tablespoon of the oil until golden brown. Lift out into a casserole and fry the onions in the remaining oil. Add the onions, soup, stock, bay leaf, salt, pepper and the liquid from the canned flageolets, to the rabbit. Cover and bake in a moderately hot oven (375°F, 190°C, Gas Mark 5) for 1 hour and 30 minutes. Remove the rabbit joints. Mix the cornflour with a little cold water and stir into the liquid in the casserole. Put back rabbit joints, pour sauce over the rabbit and add the beans. Return to the oven for 15 minutes.

Melon balls in wine

INGREDIENTS	METRIC	IMP.	U.S.
1 tbspn mint leaves			
1 tspn finely grated lime rind			
Sugar	*50 g*	*2 oz*	*$\frac{1}{4}$ cup*
White wine	*250 ml*	*8 fl oz*	*1 cup*
Lime juice	*50 ml*	*2 fl oz*	*$\frac{1}{4}$ cup*
Mixed melon balls [cantaloupe, honeydew]	*450 g*	*1 lb*	*1 lb*

Crush the mint leaves with the lime rind, stir in sugar. Add the wine and lime juice and stir to dissolve the sugar fully. Allow to stand for 15 minutes. Strain the syrup over the melon balls in a glass serving dish and chill for at least 30 minutes.

Melon cocktails
Cheesey topped fish
Israeli carrot salad

Melon cocktails

INGREDIENTS	METRIC	IMP.	U.S.
1 small Ogen [canteloupe] melon			
Lychees	*225 g*	*8 oz*	*1 cup*
4 pieces stem ginger			
2 tbspns ginger syrup			

Cut the melon in half, remove seeds and scoop out flesh with a melon baller. Reserve the juices. Peel the lychees and slice the stem ginger. Mix together the melon juice with the ginger syrup. Divide the fruit between three small glass dishes, pour over the syrup and decorate with the sliced ginger. Serves 3.

Fresh fruit cocktails often serve two purposes. They are less heavy on calories than other starters and eliminate the need to serve a sweet course. Some fruits always in season like melon and citrus fruits can be combined with interesting newcomers such as fresh lychees, satsumas and mangoes. The syrup can be given character by the addition of lime juice, white wine or vermouth.

Israeli carrot salad

INGREDIENTS	METRIC	IMP.	U.S.
4 large carrots			
2 oranges			
Salt and pepper			
1 tbspn oil			
Sprig of watercress			

Peel or scrape the carrots according to age, and grate coarsely. Remove the rind from both oranges and squeeze the juice from one orange. Beat in the orange rind, salt and pepper to taste and the oil. Pour the dressing over the grated carrot and chill, covered, in the refrigerator. Meanwhile, peel and divide the other orange into segments. Serve the carrot salad decorated with the fresh orange segments and garnish with a sprig of watercress. Serves 3.

Cheesey-topped fish

INGREDIENTS	METRIC	IMP.	U.S.
3 portions white fish			
Grated Cheddar cheese	*100 g*	*4 oz*	*1 cup*
Flour	*25 g*	*1 oz*	$\frac{1}{4}$ *cup*
2 tbspns Thousand Island Dressing			
Sprigs of parsley			

Arrange the fish in an ovenproof dish. Combine the cheese, flour, and dressing together to form a paste. Spread one third of the mixture over each fish portion. Bake in a moderate oven (325°F, 170°C, Gas Mark 3) for 25-30 minutes, until the fish flakes easily when tested with a fork. Serve garnished with parsley. Serves 3.

Cheddar cheese soup
Fish with paprika rice
Tossed green salad
Bramble snow

Cheddar cheese soup

INGREDIENTS	METRIC	IMP.	U.S.
3 tbspns grated [minced] onion			
3 tbspns grated [minced] carrot			
Butter	*40 g*	*1½ oz*	*3 tbspns*
Chicken stock [broth]	*1 litre+*	*2 pints*	*5 cups*
½ tspn dry mustard			
½ tspn paprika pepper			
Milk	*150 ml*	*¼ pint*	*½ cup*
2 tbspns cornflour [cornstarch]			
Grated Cheddar cheese	*100 g*	*4 oz*	*1 cup*
Salt and pepper to taste			
2 tbspns chopped parsley			

Sauté the onion and carrot in the butter over low heat for 10 minutes. Add the chicken stock, mustard, and paprika, and simmer for 15 minutes. Combine the milk and cornflour. Add to the pan and cook, stirring constantly until mixture thickens. Simmer for 4 minutes. Add the cheese and stir until it is melted. Season to taste and serve garnished with parsley.

Fish with paprika rice

INGREDIENTS	METRIC	IMP.	U.S.
Cod fillet	*450 g*	*1 lb*	*1 lb*
Lemon juice			
Salt and pepper			
Chicken stock [broth]	*600 ml*	*1 pint*	*2½ cups*
Long grain rice	*225 g*	*8 oz*	*½ lb*
1 tbspn paprika pepper			
Canned tomatoes	*225g*	*8 oz*	*1 cup*

Cut the fish into pieces and sprinkle with lemon juice and salt. Pour the stock into a saucepan, bring to the boil and add the fish, rice, paprika and pepper. Drain the tomatoes and stir the liquid into the rice. Bring back to the boil, stir once, cover and simmer gently for 15 minutes, or until the rice and fish are tender and the liquid absorbed. Chop the tomatoes roughly, stir into the rice mixture and reheat. Check seasoning, adjust if necessary, and serve with a tossed green salad.

Bramble snow

INGREDIENTS	METRIC	IMP.	U.S.
Cooking apples	*225 g*	*8 oz*	*½ lb*
Blackberries	*225 g*	*8 oz*	*½ lb*
Water	*150 ml*	*¼ pint*	*½ cup*
2 tspns gelatine [gelatin]			
2 egg whites			
Chopped nuts to decorate			

Chop the apples and stew with the blackberries in the water until soft. Sieve to remove the seeds. Dissolve the gelatine in 2 tablespoons water in a basin over a pan of hot water. Stir into the purée. When beginning to set, fold in the two egg whites, stiffly whisked. Pour into a glass dish and allow to set. Sprinkle chopped nuts round the edge of the dish before serving.

Saffron fish soup with toasties
Eggs in tomato concasse
Fresh plums and pears

Saffron fish soup

INGREDIENTS	METRIC	IMP.	U.S.
1 head fennel			
3 medium onions			
1 clove garlic			
2 tbspns oil			
Salt and pepper			
1 bay leaf			
½ tspn dried thyme			
White wine	*150 ml*	*¼ pint*	*½ cup*
Cod fillet	*750 g*	*1½ lb*	*1½ lb*
Water	*½ litre*	*1 pint*	*2½ cups*
Pinch powdered saffron			
Large strip orange rind			

Trim and finely chop the fennel, onions and garlic and sauté in the oil until softened but not browned. Season with salt and pepper, and add the bay leaf, thyme and wine. Skin the fish, cut into chunks and add to the pan with the water, saffron and orange rind. Cook over gentle heat covered for 45 minutes. Remove orange rind and bay leaf and serve hot with toasties.

To make toasties, thinly slice a French stick and spread the slices on a baking sheet. Put in a cool oven, or use up residual oven heat after baking, until the slices are golden brown, crisp and brittle. Store in an airtight container until required.

Eggs in tomato concasse

INGREDIENTS	METRIC	IMP.	U.S.
4 eggs			
Butter	*25 g*	*1 oz*	*2 tbspns*
1 tspn oil			
1 clove garlic			
1 medium onion, chopped			
4 medium tomatoes			
1 tbspn tomato purée [paste]			
1 tspn sugar			
1 tspn dried thyme			
2 bay leaves			
Salt and pepper			
Grated Gruyère cheese	*40 g*	*1½ oz*	*⅓ cup*

Hard-boil the eggs and shell them. Meanwhile heat the butter and oil and use to cook the crushed garlic and chopped onion gently until soft. Chop the tomatoes and add to the pan with the tomato purée, sugar, herbs, bay leaves and seasoning to taste. Simmer gently, covered, until very thick, but do not allow to burn. Pass through a sieve. Divide the mixture between four ramekin dishes, gently lower the eggs into the ramekins, sprinkle with cheese and place under a hot grill until the cheese begins to melt.

Moorish-style sausages with side dishes
Chicory and orange salad

Moorish-style sausages

INGREDIENTS	METRIC	IMP.	U.S.
Beef sausages [beef links]	*450 g*	*1 lb*	*1 lb*
1 medium onion			
Natural [plain] yogurt	*300 ml*	$\frac{1}{2}$ *pint*	$1\frac{1}{4}$ *cups*
Grated rind and juice of $\frac{1}{2}$ *lemon*			
$\frac{1}{2}$ *tspn ground ginger*			
1 tspn curry powder			
1 tbspn chopped mint			
Salt and pepper			

Place the sausages in a shallow dish. Finely chop the onion and mix with yogurt, lemon rind and juice, ginger, curry powder, mint and seasoning to taste. Pour over the sausages, cover and chill for 12 hours. Remove the sausages from the marinade and grill (broil) for 15-20 minutes, turning occasionally, until golden brown and cooked through. Heat the remaining marinade to boiling point. Skewer the cooked sausages and arrange on a serving dish with their sauce. Serve with side dishes of hot lime pickle, sliced cucumber, mango chutney, roasted nuts and desiccated coconut.

Chicory and orange salad

INGREDIENTS	METRIC	IMP.	U.S.
2 large oranges			
4 heads chicory [Belgian endive]			
Natural [plain] yogurt	*150 ml*	*5 oz*	$\frac{2}{3}$ *cup*
Salt and pepper			

Grate the rind from one orange, peel and divide both oranges into segments. Trim and divide the chicory heads into separate leaves. Reserve 10 or 12 leaves for the garnish and chop the rest roughly. Place the orange segments and chopped chicory in a bowl, toss with the yogurt, and part of the grated rind, reserving a little for the garnish. Season to taste. Turn the mixture into a serving dish and push chicory leaves down the sides at regular intervals. Sprinkle the remaining orange rind on the top.

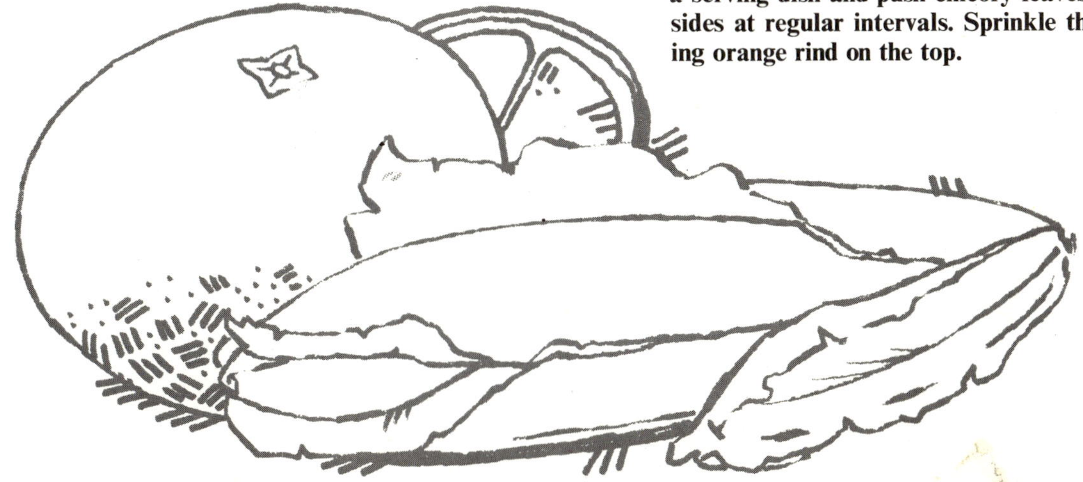

Cider-basted roast chicken
Finnish turnip loaf
Coffee mousse

Cider-basted roast chicken

INGREDIENTS	METRIC	IMP.	U.S.
Butter	*50 g*	*2 oz*	*¼ cup*
2 tbspns chopped mint and thyme			
Salt and pepper			
Roasting chicken	*1.5 kg*	*3½ lb*	*3½ lb*
Dry cider	*300 ml*	*½ pint*	*1¼ cups*
Sprig of thyme			

Soften the butter and beat in the herbs. Season well. Spread the herb butter thickly over the chicken and place any remaining inside the carcase. Place in a roasting tin, pour in the cider and roast in a moderate oven (350°F, 180°C, Gas Mark 4) for 1½ hours, basting frequently with the pan juices. Place the chicken on a warm serving dish and keep hot. Boil the pan juices rapidly until reduced by half and spoon over the chicken. Garnish with a sprig of thyme.

Finnish turnip loaf

INGREDIENTS	METRIC	IMP.	U.S.
Turnips	*450 g*	*1 lb*	*1 lb*
2 eggs			
1 tspn sugar			
Pinch pepper			
Pinch grated nutmeg			
Single cream [half & half]	*50 ml*	*2 fl oz*	*¼ cup*
4 tbspns soft breadcrumbs			
1 tbspn melted butter			

Peel, dice and cook the turnips in boiling salted water until tender. Drain and mash. Beat the eggs lightly and add to the mashed turnips along with the sugar, pepper, nutmeg and cream. Spoon into a buttered 1 lb/450 g loaf tin. Combine the breadcrumbs and melted butter. Sprinkle over the turnip mixture. Bake in a moderately hot oven (375°F, 190°C, Gas Mark 5) for 45 minutes. (In moderate oven allow 1 hour.)

Coffee mousse

INGREDIENTS	METRIC	IMP.	U.S.
2 eggs			
1 tbspn gelatine [gelatin]			
Strong black coffee	*300 ml*	*½ pint*	*1¼ cups*
Clear honey			
Little whipped cream			

Separate the eggs. Sprinkle the gelatine on the coffee in a pan. Stir over moderate heat until the gelatine has dissolved. Add a little clear honey to sweeten. Cool slightly and beat in the egg yolks. When the coffee mixture is on the point of setting, stiffly whisk the egg whites and fold in lightly. Divide between 4 small glass dishes and allow to set. Top each mousse with a swirl of whipped cream before serving.

Lemon grilled salmon trout
Cucumber sauté
Cheese and apple platter

Lemon grilled salmon trout

INGREDIENTS	METRIC	IMP.	U.S.
3 medium shallots			
Butter	*25 g*	*1 oz*	*2 tbspns*
1 tbspn cornflour [cornstarch]			
Chicken stock [broth]	*300 ml*	*½ pint*	*1¼ cups*
1 tbspn lemon juice			
1 tspn freshly chopped rosemary			
4 salmon trout steaks			
Salt and pepper			
1 tbspn melted butter			

Chop the shallots and cook in the butter until soft. Stir in the cornflour and chicken stock. Cook until thickened, stirring constantly. Stir in the lemon juice and rosemary. Keep warm. Sprinkle the fish steaks with salt and pepper and brush with the melted butter. Place on a rack and grill under medium heat for 15 minutes, turning once, or until the flesh flakes easily with a fork. Transfer to a warm serving dish. Pour the lemon shallot sauce over the fish steaks.
***Note:* The sauce can be served with whole trout.**

Cucumber sauté

INGREDIENTS	METRIC	IMP.	U.S.
2 medium cucumbers			
Cooked new potatoes	*225 g*	*8 oz*	*½ lb*
Flour	*40 g*	*1½ oz*	*⅓ cup*
Salt and pepper			
Butter	*50 g*	*2 oz*	*¼ cup*
1 tbspn chopped parsley			
Lemon slices			

Peel and cut the cucumbers into ½ inch/1 cm cubes. Cube the potatoes. Season the flour with salt and pepper. Toss the diced potato and cucumber in the seasoned flour. Fry the vegetables in the melted butter until nicely browned, about 15 minutes. Add the chopped parsley. Arrange in a hot serving dish and garnish with the lemon slices.

Spinach-cheese ramekins
Mackerel in foil parcels
Orange vegetable purée

Spinach-cheese ramekins

INGREDIENTS	METRIC	IMP.	U.S.
Spinach	*450 g*	*1 lb*	*1 lb*
Cooked long-grain rice	*100 g*	*4 oz*	*1 cup*
Grated Cheddar cheese	*125 g*	*4 oz*	*1 cup*
2 eggs			
Milk	*150 ml*	*¼ pint*	*½ cup*
Pinch dried oregano			
Salt and pepper			
2 tbspns grated Parmesan cheese			

Cook the spinach in a small amount of boiling salted water for 3 minutes. Drain and squeeze out any moisture then chop finely. Butter 4 ramekin dishes and alternate layers of chopped spinach, cooked rice, and Cheddar cheese, ending with a layer of spinach. Beat the eggs with the milk and seasonings. Pour over the spinach mixture. Sprinkle the Parmesan cheese on top. Set the ramekin dishes in a pan of hot water, bake in a moderately hot oven (375°F, 190°C, Gas Mark 5) for 25-30 minutes or until crisp and brown on top. Serve hot.

Mackerel in foil parcels

INGREDIENTS	METRIC	IMP.	U.S.
4 mackerel			
Butter	*25 g*	*1 oz*	*2 tbspns*
Juice and grated rind of 1 lemon			
1 onion, sliced in thin rings			
1 tbspn chopped parsley			
Lemon wedges to garnish			

Clean the fish and cut off the heads and tails. Place each fish on a piece of foil about 8 inches/ 20 cm square, or to suit the size of the fish. Spread a little butter inside each fish, with a few drops of lemon juice. Top with a few onion rings and a little grated lemon rind. Sprinkle with chopped parsley and enclose the fish in the foil to make firm watertight parcels. Place on a baking sheet and cook in a moderate oven (350°F, 180°C, Gas Mark 4) for 30-35 minutes. Serve from the parcels, and garnish with lemon wedges.

Orange vegetable purée

INGREDIENTS	METRIC	IMP.	U.S.
Cooked carrots	*100 g*	*4 oz*	*½ cup*
Cooked swede [rutabaga]	*450 g*	*1 lb*	*2 cups*
Orange juice	*2 tbspns*	*2 tbspns*	*3 tbspns*
2 tspns finely grated orange rind			
Salt and pepper			
Butter	*15 g*	*½ oz*	*1 tbspn*
1 egg yolk			

Mash the carrots and swede until smooth and beat in the orange juice, grated rind and seasoning to taste. Place in a small saucepan with the butter and reheat, stirring all the time. Beat in the egg yolk, remove from the heat and keep warm.

Fish and pasta florentine
Chicken with black olive sauce
Walnut side salad

Fish and pasta florentine

INGREDIENTS	METRIC	IMP.	U.S.
3 hard-boiled eggs			
Small pasta shapes	*175 g*	*6 oz*	*1 cup*
Savoury white sauce	*450 ml*	*¾ pint*	*2 cups*
Flaked cooked smoked haddock [finnan haddie]	*175 g*	*6 oz*	*¾ cup*
Peeled prawns [large shrimp]	*50 g*	*2 oz*	*¼ cup*
Salt and pepper			
Cooked chopped spinach	*225 g*	*8 oz*	*1 cup*
Grated cheese	*50 g*	*2 oz*	*½ cup*

Chop the eggs. Cook the pasta shapes in boiling salted water until just tender. Drain and mix with the egg, sauce, fish and prawns. Season to taste. Divide the spinach between 4 ovenproof dishes and top with the fish mixture. Sprinkle with cheese and bake in a moderately hot oven (375°F, 190°C, Gas Mark 5) for 20 minutes.

Chicken with black olive sauce

INGREDIENTS	METRIC	IMP.	U.S.
4 chicken portions			
5 tbspns oil			
Salt and pepper			
Tomatoes	*450 g*	*1 lb*	*1 lb*
Black olives	*75 g*	*3 oz*	*½ cup*
1 large mild onion, chopped			
2 chicken stock [bouillon] cubes			
½ tspn dried oregano			
1 tspn sugar			
½ tspn celery salt			
3 bay leaves			
½ tspn paprika pepper			
Water	*150 ml*	*¼ pint*	*⅔ cup*
1 tbspn cornflour [cornstarch]			

Brush the chicken portions with some of the oil, sprinkle with salt and pepper and cook under a medium hot grill for 25-35 minutes, turning frequently. Meanwhile, peel the tomatoes and chop them if large. Stone and halve the olives. Cook the onion gently in the remaining oil until limp, stirring, for 2 minutes. Add the tomatoes, olives, crumbled cubes, oregano, sugar, celery salt, bay leaves, paprika and water and bring to the boil, stirring constantly. Cover and cook gently for 20 minutes. Taste and adjust seasoning. Moisten the cornflour with 2 tablespoons cold water, stir into the sauce and cook, stirring constantly until the sauce thickens. Cook for a further 2 minutes. Serve the chicken with the sauce poured over.

Walnut side salad

INGREDIENTS	METRIC	IMP.	U.S.
Seedless raisins	*25 g*	*1 oz*	*2 tbspns*
2 tbspns French [Italian] dressing			
4 slices mild onion			
1 large tomato			
White cabbage	*450*	*1 lb*	*1 lb*
Walnut halves	*50 g*	*2 oz*	*½ cup*

Soak the raisins in the salad dressing for 2 hours, until plumped. Break each slice of onion carefully into rings and finely slice the tomato. Shred the cabbage finely into a bowl and toss with the walnut halves, raisins and dressing. Divide between four individual salad bowls, top with tomato slices and onion rings.

Courgette and potato soup
Bacon and mushroom risotto
Piquant radish salad
Coconut banana whip

Courgette and potato soup

INGREDIENTS	METRIC	IMP.	U.S.
New potatoes	*225 g*	*8 oz*	*½ lb*
3 courgettes [zucchini]			
1 large onion, chopped			
Butter or margarine	*25 g*	*1 oz*	*2 tbspns*
Chicken stock [broth]	*600 ml*	*1 pint*	*2½ cups*
1 bouquet garni			
Salt and pepper			

Scrub the skins off the new potatoes and dice. Thinly slice the courgettes. Sauté the potatoes, courgettes, and onion in the butter for 5 minutes. Add the chicken stock and bouquet garni. Season with salt and pepper. Cover and simmer for 20 minutes until the vegetables are tender. Adjust seasoning, and remove bouquet garni.

Bacon and mushroom risotto

INGREDIENTS	METRIC	IMP.	U.S.
1 medium onion			
1 medium red pepper			
Button mushrooms	*100 g*	*4 oz*	*¼ lb*
2 tbspns oil			
Chopped bacon	*175 g*	*6 oz*	*1 cup*
Long grain rice	*225 g*	*8 oz*	*1 cup*
Chicken stock [broth]	*600 ml*	*1 pint*	*2½ cups*
Salt and pepper			
3 tbspns cooked peas			
2 tbspns chopped parsley			
Grated Parmesan cheese			

Chop the onion, deseed and chop the pepper and slice the mushrooms. Fry the onion gently in the oil with the bacon for 4 minutes. Add the rice and cook gently for 2-3 minutes, stirring all the time. Gradually add the stock and the seasoning and bring to boiling point. Stir in the pepper and mushroom. Cover the pan and simmer for 15 minutes, or until the rice is cooked and the liquid absorbed. Stir in the peas and parsley and serve hot, sprinkled with Parmesan cheese.

Coconut banana whip

INGREDIENTS	METRIC	IMP.	U.S.
Desiccated [shredded] coconut	*50 g*	*2 oz*	*⅔ cup*
2 large bananas			
1 tbspn clear honey			
Natural [plain] yogurt	*300 ml*	*½ pint*	*1¼ cups*

Place the coconut on a sheet of foil and toast until golden brown. Cool. Mash the bananas with the honey until smooth. Gradually mix in the yogurt and place in a glass serving dish. Sprinkle the surface with the toasted coconut just before serving.

Piquant radish salad

INGREDIENTS	METRIC	IMP.	U.S.
1 medium bunch red radishes			
4 stalks celery			
Cottage cheese	*50 g*	*2 oz*	*¼ cup*
Natural [plain] yogurt	*150 ml*	*¼ pint*	*½ cup*
1 tbspn chopped parsley			
Pinch paprika pepper			
1 tbspn lemon juice			
1 tspn sugar			
Salt and pepper			
4 lettuce leaves			

Slice the radishes and celery thinly. Blend the cottage cheese with the yogurt until smooth. Stir in the parsley, paprika, lemon juice and sugar. Season to taste with salt and pepper. Toss the sliced radishes and celery in the dressing until well coated. Chill to blend the flavours. To serve, spoon into the lettuce cups.

Fresh potted salmon
Crunchy cabbage salad
Italian pasta toss
Festive beansprout salad
Chilled gooseberry soufflé

Fresh potted salmon

INGREDIENTS	METRIC	IMP.	U.S.
Fresh salmon	*225 g*	*8 oz*	*$\frac{1}{2}$ lb*
Dry white wine	*50 ml*	*2 fl oz*	*$\frac{1}{4}$ cup*
Water	*75 ml*	*3 fl oz*	*$\frac{1}{3}$ cup*
Soft butter	*100 g*	*4 oz*	*$\frac{1}{2}$ cup*
2 tbspns mayonnaise			
Salt and pepper			
Pinch grated nutmeg			

Poach the salmon in the wine and water until it flakes easily with a fork. Drain, remove the skin and bones, and mash with a fork. Beat the butter and mayonnaise into the salmon until smooth. If the mixture is too stiff, add a little of the wine cooking liquid. Season to taste with salt, pepper and nutmeg. Spoon into a serving dish and refrigerate until serving time. Serve with lemon wedges and hot toast.

Crunchy red cabbage salad

INGREDIENTS	METRIC	IMP.	U.S.
1 small or ½ large red cabbage			
1 grapefruit			
3-4 stalks celery			
Classic French Dressing			

Shred the cabbage finely. Peel and segment the grapefruit, ensuring that all the white pith is removed. Finely slice the celery. Toss all the ingredients together with sufficient dressing to coat.

Italian pasta toss

INGREDIENTS	METRIC	IMP.	U.S.
Pasta shells	*100 g*	*4 oz*	*¼ lb*
Lean ham	*50 g*	*2 oz*	*2 slices*
1 small green pepper			
10 stuffed green olives			
½ small onion			
Italian Garlic Salad Dressing			

Cook the pasta in plenty of boiling salted water until just tender. Drain and rinse with cold water. Cut the ham into strips. Deseed and chop the pepper, slice the olives and finely chop the onion. Toss all the ingredients together with sufficient dressing to coat.

Festive beansprout salad

INGREDIENTS	METRIC	IMP.	U.S.
Beansprouts	*225 g*	*8 oz*	*½ lb*
Cranberries	*100 g*	*4 oz*	*¼ lb*
1 orange			
3 tbspns Coleslaw Salad Dressing			
1 tbspn milk			

Rinse the beansprouts in cold water and drain well. Cut the cranberries in half, reserving a few for the garnish. Peel and segment the orange, ensuring that all the white pith is removed. Toss together the beansprouts and cranberries; place in a serving dish and surround with the orange segments. Garnish with the reserved cranberries. Blend the dressing and milk together and spoon over the salad.

Chilled gooseberry soufflé

INGREDIENTS	METRIC	IMP.	U.S.
Green gooseberries	*450 g*	*1 lb*	*1 lb*
Water	*150 ml*	*¼ pint*	*½ cup*
Sugar	*50 g*	*2 oz*	*¼ cup*
4 eggs			
Castor [granulated] sugar	*50 g*	*2 oz*	*¼ cup*
1 tbspn unflavoured gelatine [gelatin]			
Double [whipping] cream	*150 ml*	*¼ pint*	*½ cup*
Chopped nuts			

Cook the gooseberries with the water and sugar until soft. Rub through a sieve. Separate the eggs and beat the egg yolks with the gooseberry purée and castor sugar. Soften the gelatine in 4 tablespoons of water. Stir over low heat to dissolve. Add to the gooseberry mixture. Chill until slightly thickened. Whisk the egg whites and the cream separately. Fold into the gooseberry mixture. Tie a double thickness of greaseproof paper around a 6 inch/15 cm soufflé dish so that it extends 3 inches/8 cm above the top of the dish. Pour the gooseberry soufflé into the prepared dish and chill until set. To serve, remove the paper and press chopped nuts around the edge of the soufflé.

Fruity avocado cups
Slimmer's Scotch eggs
Pear coleslaw

Fruity avocado cups

INGREDIENTS	METRIC	IMP.	U.S.
2 ripe avocados			
2 tbspns lemon juice			
1 grapefruit			
1 small red-skinned apple			
1 stick of celery			
5 cm/2 inch length cucumber			
Soured cream	*150 ml*	$\frac{1}{4}$ *pint*	$\frac{1}{2}$ *cup*
1 tbspn clear honey			

Cut the avocados in half and remove the stones. Scoop out most of the flesh from the shells and cut into cubes. Place in a bowl and sprinkle with a little of the lemon juice. Brush the edges of the avocado shells with more lemon juice. Peel and segment the grapefruit, core and dice the apple and chop the celery and cucumber. Add all these to the bowl and mix well. Spoon back into the avocado shells. Mix the soured cream, honey and the rest of the lemon juice together and spoon over the tops.

Slimmer's Scotch eggs

INGREDIENTS	METRIC	IMP.	U.S.
Pork sausagemeat [bulk pork sausage]	*225 g*	*8 oz*	*½ lb*
1 tbspn seasoned flour			
Oil and butter			
4 hard-boiled eggs			
Lettuce leaves			
4 tbspns mayonnaise			
Few drained capers			
Sprigs of watercress			
Lemon wedges			

Divide sausagemeat into 4 and flatten each piece into a 'cake'. Dust in seasoned flour and fry on both sides in a mixture of oil and melted butter. Cool. Slice the eggs and arrange a few slices, overlapping, on each sausage cake. Serve on a bed of lettuce leaves with a topping of mayonnaise. Garnish with capers, watercress and lemon wedges.

Pear coleslaw

INGREDIENTS	METRIC	IMP.	U.S.
Firm white cabbage	*225 g*	*8 oz*	*½ lb*
1 small onion			
1 medium carrot			
3 tbspns salad cream [dressing]			
Salt and pepper			
1 ripe pear			

Finely shred the cabbage into a bowl. Grate the onion and carrot and add to the cabbage with the salad cream. Mix well and add salt and pepper to taste. Core and slice the pear and fold into the coleslaw just before serving.

Adding inspiration to salads

Every slimmer needs to develop an enthusiastic approach to salads. Banish the image of the limp, wilting lettuce leaf. Salads can take an infinite variety of delicious forms, so as well as the many recipes given in the menu section, here are other bright ideas. Let's start with hints on how to present salad greens at their crisp, fresh best.

Salad greens: Wash them well but carefully, since many of these vegetables intended to be eaten raw are delicate and damaged by bruising. Pat dry with paper towels, or use a salad shaker. Tear large leaves into pieces rather than cutting them, unless to be used as a bed of shredded lettuce. Medium-sized lettuce leaves make attractive cups in which to serve mixed salads. Washed salad greens can be stored in the refrigerator for several days in a plastic bag, preferably in a salad drawer. Never add dressing until you are about to serve a green salad and then toss gently in the dressing, using two forks or a pair of salad servers, just sufficiently to coat the surfaces. The same rules apply to watercress, although mustard and cress is better left growing in its little carton, snipped off with scissors and washed, just before serving. Store cucumbers whole as unsalted slices soon dry out, and salted slices quickly get flabby. Trim the roots and tops from radishes, leaving only a short length of stalk. Bear in mind that dressed salad which is left over will often have to be thrown away.

Other raw vegetables: Many tender raw vegetables which you are used to eating cooked would also be delicious in the form of a salad. These include finely-shredded white and red cabbage, Brussels sprouts, spinach, leeks, carrots, onions and celery. Very finely chopped raw courgettes and thinly-sliced mushrooms are delicious if marinated for a short time in your chosen salad dressing.

Herbs: Even if a salad is composed of lettuce alone, it can be transformed by sprinkling with a mixture of fresh sweet herbs, including chives, or mixed with snipped spring onions. A typical pleasant combination is parsley, mint, thyme and marjoram.

Cooked and canned vegetables: Important colour and texture contrasts can be given to green salads by adding cooked beetroot, canned artichoke hearts, bamboo shoots, water chestnuts, hearts of palm and sweetcorn kernels. All vegetables usually eaten cooked are delicious if not overcooked and served cold with a salad dressing, except perhaps cabbage. Cold sauerkraut, however, is very good indeed. Cooked dried beans of various colours add calories but give pretty colour accents.

Fruit: All firm fresh fruits combine well with zingy salad dressings, lightly-cooked rhubarb included. Avoid using soft squashy berries like raspberries. Cooked fruit, especially canned, is not very successful. Some firm canned fruits such as peaches and pineapple are good and so are well-drained citrus fruits such as grapefruit.

Salad dressings: While low-calorie dressings are best for slimmers, salad meals are usually low enough in calorie content to allow a little generosity with the dressing ingredients. When you make a classic French dressing, reverse the proportions of 2 parts oil to 1 part vinegar. Experiment with yogurt as an ingredient for dressings and give it a touch of excitement with a pinch of dry mustard or curry powder. Thin down thick mayonnaise with yogurt and stir in chopped capers to save a few calories. Add grated lemon or orange rind and the juice of the fruit to your dressings. Pineapple juice is also sharp enough to please the palate. To give your dressings more 'bite', add a little chopped pickled cucumber or liquid from a piccallili jar.

Finishing touches: Tomatoes, either sliced or cut into wedges, give the touch of colour which is missing from an all-green salad. It is easy to separate the yolk from the white of a hard-boiled egg. Sprinkle on the finely-chopped white, or press the yolk through a sieve over the salad. For special occasions, just a few cubes of stale bread fried golden brown in oil and sprinkled with garlic salt could be used as a topping, or slivers of avocado coated in lemon juice so they will not turn brown. Beansprouts are well known to most cooks but the new sprouting seeds provide interesting variations. They take only a few days to grow in a jar in the kitchen.

Moulded vegetable salad: Dissolve 1 tablespoon gelatine (gelatin) in 4 tablespoons water in a basin over a pan of hot water. Stir in 450 ml/$\frac{3}{4}$ pint/1$\frac{3}{4}$ cups chicken stock, 1 teaspoon Worcestershire sauce and 225 g/8 oz/1 cup mixed cooked vegetables such as diced carrot, sliced green beans, sweetcorn kernels and peas. Season to taste and allow to stand until the mixture begins to thicken. Stir well and pour into an oiled mould. Chill until set, turn out and serve wedges of the salad with cold ham and cottage cheese cornets.

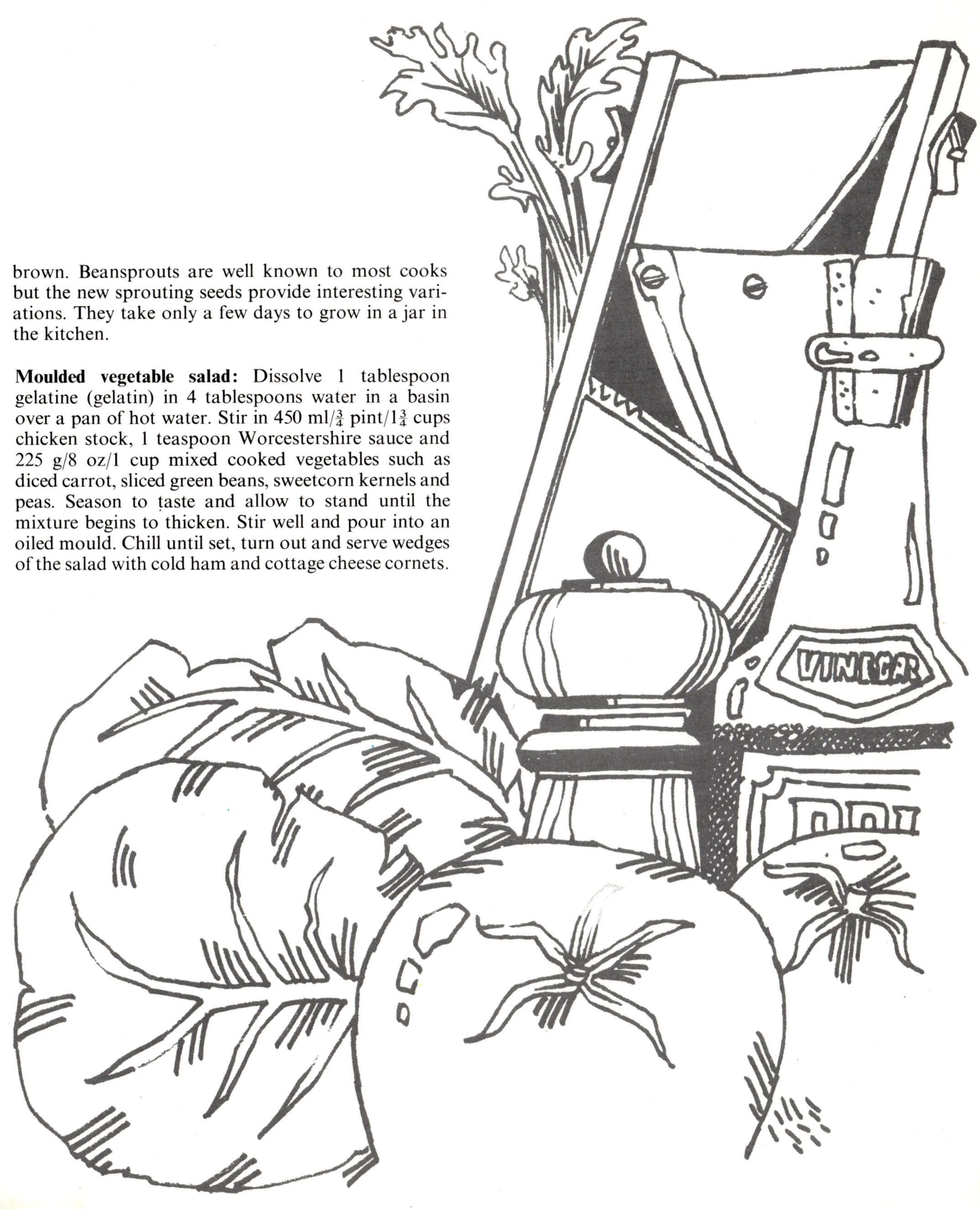

Acknowledgments

The author and publishers thank the following for their help in supplying photographs for this book, some of which were adapted from Four Seasons Cookery:

John Lee Studio
Roy Rich, Angel Studio
Christian Delu
White Fish Kitchen, p. 16-17
Tabasco Pepper Sauce, p. 18-19
Summer Avocados, p. 20-21
Kraft Foods Ltd., p. 22-23, p. 70-71, p. 86-87
Olives From Spain, p. 28-29, p. 36-37, p. 40-41, p. 44-45
Carmel, p. 28-29
Papino Pawpaws, p. 30-31
The National Dairy Council, p. 30-31
The U.S. Rice Council, p. 32-33, p. 46-47, p. 50-51, p. 64-65, p. 72-73
The Swiss Cheese Union, Inc., p. 42-43
Californian Wine Institute, p. 42-43
New Zealand Lamb Information Bureau, p. 44-45
John West Foods, p. 52-53
The Pasta Information Centre, p. 54-55, p. 82-83
Green Giant, p. 56-57
Hassy Perfection Celery, p. 58-59
Princes Foods Ltd., p. 64-65
The Mushroom Information Bureau, p. 66-67
Baxters of Speyside, p. 68-69
Farmhouse English Cheddar, p. 72-73
The British Sausage Bureau, p. 76-77, p. 88-89
Taunton Cider Co. p. 78-79
British Bacon Bureau, p. 84-85
Gales Honey, p. 88-89

Index